Indo-Mal[ay]
Martial Traditions

Aesthetics, Mysticism, & Combatives

Vol. 1

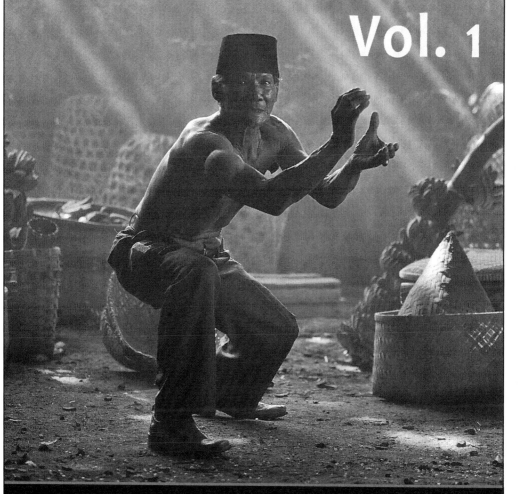

An Anthology of Articles from the *Journal of Asian Martial Arts*

Edited by Michael A. DeMarco, M.A.

Copyright © 2015 by
Via Media Publishing Company
941 Calle Mejia #822
Santa Fe, NM 87501 USA
E-mail: md@goviamedia.com

All articles in this anthology were originally published in the *Journal of Asian Martial Arts*. Listed according to the table of contents for this anthology:

Davies, P. H. J. (2000)   Volume 9, Number 2   pages 28–47
Wilson, J. (1993)   Volume 2, Number 2   pages 10–43
Wiley, M. (1994)   Volume 3, Number 4   pages 38–45
Pauka, K. (1995)   Volume 4, Number 3   pages 26–45

Book and cover design by Via Media Publishing Company

Edited by Michael A. DeMarco, M.A.

Cover illustration
Artwork © Pop Vichaya
Facebook.com/Pop315Photography

ISBN: 978-1-893765-21-4

www.viamediapublishing.com

contents

preface

There seem to be more martial art styles in Southeast Asia than the number of islands in the region—and the Indonesian archipelago alone has 18,307 islands. We really don't know how many forms of silat are presently being practiced in Indonesia and Malaysia. Many arts are kept private, taught in secluded areas away from the public. These are arts of the older tradition, developed when combative knowledge was valued for its use in protecting the sanctity of life.

Popular martial arts in the Indo-Malay area reflect modern perspectives and interests, often exuding a competitive sport climate or simply serving as forms of athletic and aesthetic display. Taekwondo is one such popular art. But this two-volume anthology brings together a great collection of writings by authors who dive into the deepest realms of Indo-Malay combatives. They offer readers a rare viewing of martial traditions that is usually hidden behind social shrouds of secrecy and a clannish quest to preserve individual tradition.

The Indo-Malay area has been greatly impacted by waves of Indian, Arab, and Chinese immigrations. The influences are clearly visible in the religious and social realms, and in the unique blending of martial traditions. Dr. Philip Davies masterfully details the complex social milieu in the Indo-Malay martial tradition with a focus on the Chinese arts referred to by the ambiguous term *kuntao*. His writing underlines the importance of martial arts to specific social groups, and what and how these groups practice these combative forms.

As an initiate into the art of Bimi Sakti, James Wilson penetrates into the heart of Javanese silat and shares the deeper significance of what the practice means to the indigenous culture. His chapter illustrates how beliefs and practices entwine, especially with the animistic roots of Indonesia. The influence makes Javanese silat unique in practice as well as social standing.

A main ingredient in Southeast Asian silat styles is *kebatinan*: "the science of the inner." Mark Wiley's chapter details the place of kebatinan in the culture and martial tradition. The blend of ancient animistic beliefs and mystical religions has given a psychological charge to silat's methods as a source of mystical power.

Dr. Kirstin Pauka's chapter brings together many aspects of silat in a report on a rare celebration—the Pauleh Tinggi ceremony. This three-day event occurs only when the social needs arise and may not occur again for decades. She was fortunate to be in West Sumatra for this occasion, equipped with strong academic skills and experience to extract the significance of the ceremony. Silat performances by individuals, pairs, and groups are the primary features and go on throughout each day and night. Descriptions of the mental and physical sides of the silat performances offer readers an exclusive view of a martial tradition in which combative skills flow from an inner mystical guidance that vitalize the movements. The psychic state is embodied in both the art as well as social relationships.

All who are serious about the history and practice of Indo-Malay fighting arts will enjoy this special anthology, volumes 1 and 2. We are very fortunate to assemble the works of these highly qualified authors. Each chapter is a gem. We hope reading will provide information you seek. Although true silat masters are nearly impossible to find, the chapters here will certainly add direction and inspiration for practitioners.

Michael A. DeMarco
Santa Fe, New Mexico
November 2015

author bio notes

Philip H. J. Davies, Ph.D., received his degree in sociology from the University of Reading in England, and a postgraduate certificate from Brunel University in London. He is the cofounder and director of the Brunel Centre for Intelligence and Security Studies at Brunel University. Dr. Davies began studying Kuntao Matjan under Richard Kudding in 1981 and continues to train. Kuntao Matjan, from Central Java, combines Indonesian pencak silat with a form of Southern Chinese tiger-style gongfu. It was brought to the West by the late Dutch Indonesian master Carel Faulhaber and is currently headed by his closest student, Richard Kudding. The UK representative is Dr. Davies. The art is recognized with the International Pencak Silat Federation in Jakarta.

Kirstin Pauka, Ph.D., received her degree from Justus Liebig Universität in Germany and is now a professor in the Department of Theatre and Dance at the University of Hawai'i at Manoa. She has served as an associate editor for the *Journal of Asian Martial Arts*, and authored four articles dealing with Indonesian martial arts. Other works include *Theater & Martial Arts in West Sumatra: Randai & Silek of the Minangkabau* (Ohio University Press, 1999) and, on CD-ROM, *Randai: Folk Theater, Dance, and Martial Arts of West Sumatra* (University of Michigan Press, 2002). Dr. Pauka practices Japanese taiko drumming and trains in aikido, taekwondo, and silek. www.ohioswallow.com/author/Kirstin+Pauka

Mark V. Wiley, B.A., received his bachelor of arts degree in sociology from Drexel University. He began martial arts training in 1979 and has focused on Cabales Serrada Escrima under Grandmaster Angel Cabales. As an author, Wiley's works include *Filipino Martial Arts: Cabales Serrada Escrima* (Tuttle 1994) and *Filipino Fighting Arts: Theory and Practice* (Unique 2000). He has worked in the publishing field, including Tuttle Publishing and CFW Enterprises, and now is self-employed with Tambuli Media.

James Wilson, J.D., Dip. Ac./Lic. Ac., has a dual juris doctor degree from Georgetown University Law Center (juris doctor and master of science in foreign service) and is a licensed graduate of the New England School of Acupuncture. Fluent in Bahasa Indonesia, he went to Indonesia to study a pencak silat style called Bima Sakti under Guru Besar Pak F. L. Siswanto in Central Java.

What is Kuntao?
Cultural Marginality in the
Indo-Malay Martial Arts Tradition
by Philip H.J. Davies, Ph.D.

Liu Sheong (right) in Indonesia practicing kuntao with his nephew Willem Reeders (left)
was one of the earlier kuntao practitioners to immigrate to the United States
to teach a variety of styles. Photo courtesy of Richard Lopez.

All margins are dangerous.
—Douglas, 1979: 121

Introduction[1]

Roughly speaking, there are three main classes of martial art that derive from the shared Indonesian and Malaysian cultural and linguistic tradition (referred to hereafter as the Nusantara tradition;[2] silat or pencak silat, pukulan, and kuntao.[3] To a certain degree, the use of these terms is ambiguous, as much among native speakers of the various Nusantara languages as among Western commentators. However, a rough distinction can be drawn between them.

In general terms, silat refers to a class of combative system which is deeply interwoven with the broader culture of Nusantara society, usually including both fighting and performance arts and generally incorporating elements of traditional

1

musical and dance conventions into the fighting style. Pukulan is a less clear-cut matter, refering to another class of systems characterized by structural and pedagogical simplicity and a minimum of institutional formalization.[4] While silat and pukulan are particular to the Indo-Malay mainstream of Nusantara culture and history, the term "kuntao" refers to a broad range of arts that straddle the boundary between that mainstream and the 'Overseas Chinese' community (or rather, communities) that have grown up within the geographical expanse subsumed under the idea of the Nusantara. Because of that marginality between two profoundly different yet geographically proximate identities, the status and therefore the future of the "kuntao" class of arts is a far more uncertain one than that faced by either of the two indigenous traditions.

The issue of what the term "kuntao" refers to, and what it means, and the implications of these factors for understanding the history and status of kuntao have become an increasingly fraught matter in the western martial arts community because of the number of kuntao systems brought to the west by emigre Dutch-Indonesians during the 1950's. There has been a failure to find a generally agreed conclusion in western literature. The following analysis will seek to demonstrate that even as used by native speakers of the Nusantara languages and dialects, the notion of "kuntao" is profoundly ambiguous. In part, that ambiguity reflects a fundamental cultural distinction within the Chinese peoples resident in Indonesia, Malaysia, Singapore, and Brunei-Darussalam. That distinction is between two attitudes to cultural marginality adopted by emigre Chinese in Southeast Asia.

On the one hand, there are the orthodox Chinese who remain relatively insular in lifestyle, seeking to maintain or replicate the cultural and social context of China within their overseas communities. On the other hand, there are partially or completely integrated ethnic Chinese populations that, while identifiable by the use of Chinese names and any distinguishing physical traits (e.g. supposedly lighter skin) from the majority indigenous peoples (*bumiputra*, sometimes *pribumi*), adopt local language, etiquette, and sometimes even the prevalent religion where they have settled.[5] In another part, the ambiguity of the notion is a consequence of the degrees to which ideas, methods and skills travel across, or even hover on the boundaries of the interfaces between these two strains or ethnic Chinese in Southeast Asia, and between the various ethnic Chinese groups and the bumiputra majority.

Any attempt to understand what is meant by kuntao must, therefore, be grounded in the distinction between orthodox and integrated Chinese sub-communities and the social causes and consequences of cultural marginality. What will become apparent, therefore, is that much of the confusion and inconsistency in western discussions of what kuntao is, or is not, and what it may or may not mean, is not merely a consequence of a cross-cultural failure on the part of Western commentators to understand the matter, but in fact reflects an intrinsic ambiguity and uncertainty that exists within the indigenous use of the term "kuntao" within the Nusantara. Above and beyond any conceptual issues, however, a direct consequence of that indigenous ambiguity means that the future propagation and survival of the kuntao category of martial arts is a far more fraught matter than are the unambiguously indigenous arts of silat and pukulan.

The Nusantara Chinese: Peranakan and Totok

The Chinese are possibly the single most widespread, visible ethnic minority group in Southeast Asia. Their role in the region has typically been that of traders along the coasts in the larger towns and cities, although in the Malay peninsula one can also find inland Hokkien Chinese who have historically made up the labor force in the old tin mines during the British Empire period. In Malaysia, ethnic Chinese make up 32% or more of the population, while in Indonesia (at least prior to the 1998 riots and subsequent exodus to neighboring states such as Malaysia and Singapore), the ethnic Chinese only make up around 2.8% of the population—although in a state as populous as Indonesia, that still amounts to around six million people.

There is also a long history of ethnic strife and hostility between the Chinese and the indigenous peoples of the Nusantara (bumiputra) despite, or perhaps partly because of, the frequent reliance of Nusantara monarchies upon the wealth and financial management of Chinese businessmen kept on retainers to the court, or who at least cooperate with the court in trade and development (Suryadinata, 1997: 8, 23–74; Geertz, 1980: 38–39, 94–97). Among less tolerant bumiputra, the Chinese are sometimes referred to as "the Jews of Asia," which coming from some more orthodox Muslims achieves a disturbingly double-edged racism. During the Suharto administration (1967–1999), there was also a long history of anti-Chinese policy and sentiment, supposedly arising out of the role of the Chinese (and Mainland Chinese) sponsorship of the 1965 "generals' coup." Anti-Chinese legislation included the banning of Chinese language publications, including street signs, the public display of Chinese traditions and celebrations, and the requirement that ethnic Chinese adopt Indonesian names in order to hold full citizenship. Of course, during the recent Asian financial crisis, hostility between bumiputra and ethnic Chinese has escalated until it peaked with the now notorious 1998 riots and alleged organized rapes in urban centers like Jakarta and Surabaya.

However, such a clear division between bumiputra and ethnic Chinese is an oversimplification. There has been an ongoing influx of ethnic Chinese into the region for centuries, and so, unsurprisingly, there has been a history of progressive integration of ethnic Chinese groups and individuals into the Nusantara culture and society. Roughly speaking, the Nusantara Chinese can be divided into two distinct groups. One group is highly integrated into Nusantara society and is referred to as the Peranakan Chinese.[6]

Peranakan Chinese generally speak the indigenous language of a region, e.g. Indonesian, Javanese, Sundanese, or Malay, rather than any Chinese dialect. Peranakans are sometimes also referred to as "Babah Chinese." The Peranakans trace their history to pre-colonial Chinese settlements in the major centers of the old Nusantara kingdoms. As described in Suryadinata, originally "Peranakan Chinese generally had indigenous blood from the female line and partly adopted the indigenous way of life. Their males wore the *theng-sha* (Chinese long dress) while their females dressed in *kebaya* (Indonesian dress) and were raised by their mothers. Peranakans generally spoke no Chinese but communicated in the local tongue. On the north coast of Java where most of the Chinese lived, a combination of bazaar Malay and the Hokkien dialect was used as a lingua franca. This language was later enriched by borrowings from Dutch and other Western languages. By the late nineteenth century, the language had developed into Bahasa Melajoe Betawi (Batavian Malay), known as Bahasa Melajoe Tionghua (Chinese Malay) in the present century" (Suryadinata, 1981: 2).

The Peranakan dialect was often referred to as Babah Malay in the Straits Colonies, and derisively as Babi Malay (pig Malay) among anti-Chinese Malays.[7] Although the Peranakans spoke the Nusantara languages, they generally retained Chinese names, which meant that they remained a visible minority despite linguistic and cultural integration.

The other distinct group is the Totok Chinese. Totok Chinese are more conservative than the Peranakan, and have retained their language and culture to a greater degree. For the most part, the Totoks are twentieth century immigrants. Suryadinata describes them thus: "The Totoks, being more recent migrants, are still culturally 'Chinese' in the sense that they still speak Chinese. They are China-born, and their descendents—i.e. the second generation Totoks—if they were born before World War II, are likely to remain Totok culturally, because they received Chinese education and joined Totok-dominated organizations" (Suryadinata, 1997: 9–10).

However, like any recent immigrant group, the Totoks have been subject to both conscious and unconscious integrationist pressures, partly by virtue of simply living in the Nusantara milieu, and partly also through governmental policies of integration under the Suharto administration. As a result, second-generation Totoks born during the 1960's or later have tended to be more integrated into Indonesian society than their parents (Suryadinata, 1997: 10). Suryadinata describes the process of progressive integration into Indonesian society as "Peranakanization" and "Indonesianization," that is, the second generation Totoks are increasingly absorbed into the partially integrated Peranakan community and lifestyle, while Peranakan offspring are likewise increasingly integrated into the Nusantara mainstream of Indonesian culture.

It is easy to ascribe the tensions between ethnic groups to simple, judgmental terms such as "racism," "prejudice," and even the "politics of envy." It would be very tempting to take just such a view of the tensions that exist on the frontier between the bumiputra and the Totok that the Peranakans occupy. However, just as the tendency for communities to turn upon the alien is more the rule than the exception, so too the tendency to exclude and abjure those things that lie on the boundaries between that which is within and that which is without is perhaps even more pronounced. Marginal communities are typically excluded by those on both sides of the boundary that they straddle. At one time, people of mixed African-American and Euro-American heritage could expect to be derided as "zebras." In South Africa, the "coloreds" of mixed African and White blood might have been placed above the full-blooded Africans in the apartheid chain of being, but they were shunned by black and white alike nonetheless. Likewise, in that other erstwhile Dutch colonial possession of Indonesia (1799–1949), the Dutch-Indonesians may have occupied a middle-ranking niche between fullblooded Dutch and native "inlanders," but come the revolution, they were unwelcome both in an independent Indonesia and a white, European Holland.

The problem with marginal groups is their very ambiguity, their violation of the cut-and-dried categories that people in a community use to order and make sense of their worlds, their impurity.

Anthropologist Mary Douglas has provided an elegant and adaptable diagnosis of the sense of threat that comes with categorical ambiguity. The process is not simply a social or political one, but one deeply rooted in our consciousness of the world. We perceive, understand and make sense of the world in terms of systems of categories and labels that provide "pigeonholes" in which we fit clusters of sensory "cues." "As time goes on," she writes, "and experiences pile up, we make a greater investment in our system of labels. So a conservative bias is built in. It gives us confidence" (Douglas, 1979: 36).

That confidence is crucial to the matter, because our ability to navigate our world depends on our confidence in our system of pigeonholes. But anomalous objects that violate our expectations or ambiguous ones that violate the boundaries between those pigeonholes threaten to bring the whole architecture down in chaos and confusion.

There are several ways of treating anomalies. Negatively, we can ignore, just not perceive them, or perceiving them we can condemn. Positively we can deliberately confront the anomaly and try to create a new pattern of reality in which it has a place ... A private person may revise his pattern of assumptions or not. It is a private matter. But cultural assumptions are public matters. They cannot easily be subject to revision.

—Douglas, 1979: 38–39

And, of course, the definition of self and others in terms of their membership and position with categories of community membership are amongst the most central and most crucial pigeonholes we use to define the world and our place within it.

In the political and social realm, there is a profound distinction between the universalistic notions of community membership of modem, industrial societies and the particularistic orientations and expectations of traditional societies. As Max Weber notes in his *General Economic History* (1982: 315–338), a major feature of the emergence of the cosmopolitan modem state is the evolution of notions of citizenship, defined by rights, responsibilities conformity to a general system of laws rather than a historical or ethnic identity. The difference between the "modem" (in Weber's sense) concept of "citizenship" and the "traditional" concept of identity is ultimately that a traditional identity is ultimately non-negotiable. One may in principle swear an oath of allegiance and be bound to observe a nation-state's laws almost regardless of one's ethnicity or nation-state of origin,[8] but one cannot change the color of one's skin nor unmake one's history (although one might try to ignore both, like integrated European Jews in the first half of this century). The breadth and depth of such matters are so great that even if one were to confront the anomaly, it would be prohibitively complex and costly to, as Douglas suggests, "create a new pattern of reality in which it has a place." This would involve casting asunder the entire foundation of a traditional society's self-definition, and the self-definition of its members. Therefore, the only possible options are negative ones: to ignore the anomaly, or to condemn it, and either exile it or to force it to abandon its anomalous nature and seek a conventional and unchallenging integration.

In Indonesia, pressures toward integration have come essentially from two different directions. In the first place, there has always been the relatively innocuous immersion into Nusantara culture, languages, norms, and institutions simply by virtue of living in the region. However, and perhaps more crucially, successive governments—both colonial administrations and nationalist governments—have implemented a history of policies that affected the status of the ethnic Chinese. Under the Dutch colonial government, there was a generally pervasive policy of promoting ethnic separateness, sometimes by offering Peranakans a partial citizenship not available to the bumiputra (Suryadinata, 1981: 9–13, 25–38). However, the progressive alienation of the Peranakans from the Dutch during the interwar period increasingly aligned them with Sukarno's Nationalists. As a result, after independence, the Sukarno administration (1945–1965) was relatively favorably disposed toward the Peranakans (but less so to the Totoks who had tended to align with China-centered pan-Chinese movements). Sukarno had expressed the willingness to formally recognize the Peranakans as a *suku*[9] (ethnic group) in their own right alongside the established bumiputra suku like the Javanese, Sundanese, and Batak (Suryadinata, 1997: 8), part and parcel with the national dictum of "unity and diversity" and the explicitly pluralist-nationalist state ideology of Pancasila.[10] There is even a long-standing political tradition advocating a Peranakan suku amongst the Peranakans referred to as "Baperkism."[11]

Any institutionalized tolerance or equality for the Peranakans was dispelled in the wake of the 1965 "generals' coup" that toppled Sukarno and gave rise to the more recently defunct Suharto government. Central players in the uprising that led to the coup were the Komunis Partei Indonesia (KPI), which boasted a prominent (even, according to some, prevalent) proportion of ethnic Chinese in its numbers; the Communist government in Beijing also actively supported it. By some accounts, the suppression of the 1965 uprising may have entailed as many as 200,000 ethnic Chinese deaths (Dalton 1989: 37). As a result, under the new Jakarta regime, all things Chinese were declared a threat to national security and subversive to Pancasila. Comprehensive prohibitions against Chinese organizations and cultural practices were implemented. As one commentator summarizes it:

> The government prevents Chinese from settling in rural areas in large numbers, and Chinese are not allowed to run their own schools, publish their own newspapers or form political parties. Chinese characters have been erased, by government decree, from all of Indonesia's Chinatowns and even blacked out of photographs in magazines. Chinese-language foreign publications are banned. The authorities have even outlawed "tai chi." Chinese may not keep dual citizenship and must take on Indonesian surnames. — Dalton, 1989: 37

It has to be said that the prosperous 1980's were a period of political liberalization among the Peranakans, resulting in a limited reappearance of Baperkism. By comparison, the Totok community had been hit particularly hard by the post-1965 regulations, but normalization of diplomatic relations with Beijing in 1990 eased the situation. Overall, there was a general trajectory of liberalization prior to the recent currency crisis, and the catastrophic outbreak of grass-roots level violence against the ethnic Chinese amongst the bumiputra majority. Although the distinction between Peranakan and Totok is one primarily employed in Indonesia, the gap between Babah Chinese and more orthodox communities is historically equally visible in Malaysian and Singaporean histories. In Malaysia, the distinction between Chinese and bumiputra is felt even more keenly for a number of reasons. In the first place, according to Malaysian Government statistics, ethnic Chinese (both Babah and orthodox) make up 32% of the Malaysian population, a far greater proportion of the overall population than in Indonesia. The situation is rendered considerably more fraught by Malaysia's political systems. Where Indonesia has evolved around the pluralist nationalism of Pancasila, the dominant political force in Malaysia is explicitly racial in orientation in the form of the United Malay National Organization (UMNO). The irony in Malaysia is that—with a 32% Chinese population, plus sizeable minorities of Tamil; Malayali Indians; Punjabis; and, in the northern state of Perak, a population of ethnic Thais—the Malays make up a very tenuous majority, if they still make up a majority at all.[12] On the back of this very marginal predominance, UMNO has declared Malaysia an "Islamic republic," and systematically pursues a wide variety of "positive" discriminatory measures to ensure that the bumiputra have reserved, even preferential, access to education, public services, and so forth. The result has been a tendency to erect barriers of ethnic separation at both formal and informal levels increasingly trying to marginalize the ethnic Chinese, both Babah and orthodox alike.

In Singapore, the situation is almost the complete reverse of Malaysia with the ethnic Malays being the largest minority. In this capacity, according to authors like Rahim (1998), they have been persistently "marginalised" despite a conscious government policy of multiculturalism unmatched anywhere in Southeast Asia. Although Singapore is effectively a part of the Riau Islands, and the indigenous Malays (as opposed to later immigrants from Indonesia during the Japanese occupation and after the 1965 coup) speak their own regional dialect of Melayu Riau, the dominant population is Chinese. Here the situation is even more complex than elsewhere in the Nusantara, as the Singapore Chinese are not a uniform population.

Singapore's Chinese community consists of several different ethnic sub-groups, including Hokkienese, Teochew, Hakka, Cantonese, Mandarin-speakers, and Babah, all of whom lived in linguistically uniform kampong ("small village") of their own before the present pervasive urbanization of the island took shape. Indeed, Lee Kuan Yew is a Babah from Semarang, and grew up speaking Melayu Babah rather than a Chinese dialect (Lee, 1998).

Despite the regional variations, therefore, the distinction between orthodox Chinese, or Totoks, and Babah/Peranakans is a pervasive one. This is a crucial distinction, and just as silat systems tend to be particular to specific suku bangsa, so the arts designated by the generic "kuntao" should reasonably be expected to crystallize around "sub-ethnic" groups. So, much as there are distinctions to be drawn between northern and southern Chinese martial systems; and between Hokkienese, Cantonese, and Zhezhiang "southern fist" (Man., *nanquan*) systems (among many others) within the southern Chinese tradition, one would expect to see distinctions between Totok and Peranakan arts within the Nusantara.

Peranakan and Totok Forms of Kuntao

There is a considerable degree of misunderstanding and uncertainty within the Western martial arts community concerning what kuntao systems are, or what the generic term "kuntao" refers to. For example, Draeger and Smith define kuntao as Chinese martial arts practiced within Indonesia, and only grudgingly acknowledged that "Kun-tao [sic] may have influenced pentjak-silat.... Perhaps the reverse is also true...." (1987: 184). By comparison, Bruce A. Haines is perfectly willing to gloss over the distinction between silat, pukulan, and kuntao, referring to them almost offhandedly as "variations of the same Indonesian style that have developed in different geographical areas of the Indonesian archipelago" (1968: 50). However, more recently, Bob Orlando has tended back toward the orthodox conception in referring to Chinese kuntao (Orlando, 1996).

Part of the problem is undoubtedly that of cross-cultural transition; something, somewhere, always gets lost in translation. This is made worse by the fact that one is not even dealing with a purely Indo-Malay word or idea. With the term "kuntao," one is dealing with a Nusantara idiomatic incorporation of a Chinese term, and this being a term from the major dialect (Hokkienese) perhaps least familiar to the Western world. But there is a complication more profound even than this, for the very indigenous usage of "kuntao" in the Nusantara is ambiguous even in what might be termed its "natural" context.

The most common, loose translation of "kuntao" is that it is the Hokkienese pronunciation of the Japanese term "kenpo." In this interpretation, the term "kenpo" is, of course, the Japanese reading of Chinese character for "fist" and the character for "rule" or "method," literally "fist method" and pronounced (and most familiar as) *quanfa* in Mandarin (Orlando, 1996: 123). However, this is a mistranslation because the Hokkien pronunciation of the character for rule or method is *huat*. Hence, the Hokkienese equivalent of kenpo would be *kunhuat*, not kuntao. Tao is, indeed, the Hokkien pronunciation of the character Romanized from the Mandarin as *dao* also, as in the philosophy of Daoism (and Romanized as *do* in Japanese and Korean), and meaning doctrinal path or philosophy (rather than rule or method). Of course, there are also cases of non-Chinese speaking or at least non-Chinese writing Peranakan groups that also mistranslate the term and sometimes apply the character for "stick" (or 'staff'), also pronounced "kun" (de Spa, 1997). For example, a film of the Balinese Perguruan Kun Thau Pusat school in Denpasar (taken in the 1970's by the late Thea Verschuur) clearly shows the school banner with the Chinese character for "stick" instead of the one for "fist." So it is entirely possible to find misunderstandings and uncertainties within indigenous use of the term.

"fist, boxing"   "rule method"   "stick"   "way, method"

Special thanks to Li Juan Yan
and Alan W. Ellerton for the
characters and advice on their
use and interpretations.

In its ordinary language use in Hokkienese, kuntao is used idiomatically as a generic term for martial arts, much as *quanfa, gongfu,* or *wushu* are used in Mandarin, and *kuen* or *gung fu* in Cantonese. However, in the Indonesian case, and generally throughout the Nusantara region, kuntao has been taken up in essentially two different idiomatic senses. It is these two idiomatic uses of a single term, a signifier lumbered down with at least three alternative significations, that make for the problems associated with evaluating the role and status of kuntao within the Nusantara martial tradition.

As used in Indonesia, Malaysia, and Singapore, kuntao refers to several morphologically and morphogenetically different kinds of art. For example, *Straits Times* journalist Mubin Sheppard refers to "koontao" in terms of Chinese martial arts (1983: 104). On the other hand, Malaysian silat instructor Jak Othman defines kuntao a "*seni bela diri pribumi yang telah dibungakan dengan Wushu atau Kung Fu Cina*" ("[kuntao is] a Malay art of self-defense that has been combined with Chinese wushu or gongfu"; 1999: 50). In the same periodical that Othman has employed his definition, another article by a different author quotes the guru of Kuntao Tujuh who describes kuntao as *seni silat* ("the art of silat") that is *untuk semua bangsa Melayu yang beragama Islam* ("for all Malay peoples of the Islamic faith"; Kamarrul & Amarrudin, 1999: 13). One Malay anthropologist even published a study of peninsular Malay silat using kuntao in both senses, using the Romanization "koon tao" to refer to Chinese systems and "kuntau" to refer to a particular school of silat (Rashid, 1990: 64, 66).

A kuntao school: It's worth noting that the Chinese characters do not match the English text. The typical of the regional linguistic eclecticism, the English text the school says "kuntow," but the Chinese script uses the term "guoshu." Photo courtesy of P. Davies.

There is a somewhat rarer, third idiomatic usage of the term "kuntao" in which it is employed as a broad generic for martial arts in something closer to its original Hokkienese sense. This is relatively unusual in the Nusantara language setting, but not unknown, as indicated by the fact that the Balinese system Bhakti Negara is (or, at least as late as 1973, was) colloquially referred to as Kuntao Bali. Similarly, one of the two Brunelese silat styles recognized under PERSILAT is known as Kuntao Brunei. Indonesian silat chronicler Pak O'ong Maryono discussed this third sense, noting that kuntao also appeared as a loan-word generic for self-defense arts. However, he notes, "a major linguistic change happened in the 1950s with the popularisation of the term 'silat' and gradual disappearance of the term 'kuntao,'" partly because of a shift in popular culture in which Chinese "kung fu novels" came to be written in Bahasa Indonesia and partly through the kinds of political pressures discussed above (Maryono, 2000). Suryadinata notes that the shift in the Chinese "kung fu novels" toward the language and conventions of the Indonesian "cerita silat" was itself a consequence of those same pressures (1997: 223–231). Therefore, it is evident that even within the Nusantara cultural and linguistic sphere, the notion of kuntao is a profoundly ambiguous one.

It is thus possible to speak meaningfully of three different branches or divisions of kuntao: what might be termed Totok kuntao, Peranakan kuntao, and wholly Indonesianised kuntao.[13] For the most part, Totok kuntao systems have received the lion's share of attention in Western literature, not least because of the central role of Draeger's work in Western literature on Indonesian martial arts.[14] Draeger encountered a number of different Indonesian-Chinese teachers who were involved primarily with relatively narrowly traditional Chinese styles, and for the most part his works concentrate only on narrowly traditional Chinese systems. One need only think of Tjoa Khek Kiong featured in Draeger's *Shantung Black Tiger* (1987) or a range of other figures who appear in his *Weapons and Fighting Arts of Indonesia* (1993). Such systems are "orthodox" in the sense that they retain the traditional techniques, training practice, methodologies, and, of course, language of Chinese arts. They also often retain associated traditional Chinese cultural practices and affiliations such as lion and dragon dances.

However, even as Draeger concentrates on what are herein termed Totok kuntao systems, he reports encountering a number of Indonesianized systems that have integrated themselves into the Nusantara tradition so extensively that they have even abandoned "kuntao" designation. In *Weapons and Fighting Arts of Indonesia*, he points out two systems that can be seen as indicative of Suryadinata's model of progressive integration, Perisai Sakti, and Kebudaiaan Hmu Silat Indonesia. The guru of the latter, Lie Tjie Jan, adopted an Indonesian designation for a system that Draeger evidently saw as "his obviously kuntao form . . . Little has changed insofar as kuntao mechanics and scope are concerned. The system is largely based on hand and arm tactics; kicking methods are minimal. . . . The usual weapons of kuntao are studied, and the long-bladed, single edged sword (*tao*) is the core weapon" (Draeger, 1993: 206).

By comparison, Perisai Sakti is more comprehensively eclectic but also classifies itself as a silat system. At the time that Draeger was surveying the region, the style was centered on the Chinese Catholic Youth Organization, and reportedly consists of "an interesting synthesis of Javanese pentjak-silat [sic] forms and Japanese combatives and quasi-combatives (jujutsu, judo and karatedo) superimposed on a Chinese kuntao base." Draeger further elaborates on this "kuntao base" adding in a footnote that, "positive Chinese influence from Southern China is evidenced by the use of *pei-ho* (stork style), kuntao movements, and other mechanical aspects common to Khe area (Canton) Chinese combatives. Widjiharti [the founder] is an accomplished kuntao master" (1993: 52). A similar degree of comprehensive Industrialization has taken place in the case of Pencak Silat Mustika Kwitang, although the degree and relative centrality of the Chinese influence remains a hotly disputed matter (Draeger, 1993: 86).

Therefore, what we have is a range of kuntao forms distinguished by varying degrees of integration into the Nusantara linguistic and cultural mainstream and degrees of isolation from that mainstream within the insular confines of the Totok Chinese community. The purely Totok systems and the wholly Indonesianized systems lie at the extreme; between them lies a spectrum of schools and systems that may be described as to some degree Peranakanized.

As a general rule, this process of integration involves three main factors: first, a synthesis of techniques that draws from both Chinese and Indonesian fighting lexicons; second, an adoption of Nusantara instructional and training methods; and, finally, the adoption or incorporation of kinaesthetic and performance-oriented qualities from the silat tradition (a subtle kind of change that can often be hard to describe verbally, but is often immediately apparent when the practitioners are seen in motion). One member of the Singaporean silat organization PERSISI (Persekutuan Silat Singapura) recounted a case that captured the situation perfectly. During the 1970's, Mohammad din Mohammad approached PERSISI for recognition of his art designated Kuntao Melaka (i.e. Malacca, one of the oldest and formerly one of the most powerful Malay sultanates). Despite the art's Chinese designation and evident Chinese influences (Malacca has always had one of Malaysia's largest Babah communities), Abdullah Shafiie Sidik, Deputy President of PERSISI, remarked to the present author that they could immediately "see" that Kuntao Melaka was, in its methods and movement, discernibly a "Malay art."

That there is a considerable number of these arts scattered throughout the Nusantara and among emigres and expatriates from the region is apparent even from the handful of systems that have reached the public eye. From Indonesia there come systems like Kuntao Jawa, Bangau Putih, and Bugis Makassarese, hybrids called "silat kuntao";[15] in Malaysia and Singapore there are, for example, Kontan,[16] Kuntao Melaka, and Kuntao Asli. Still others have been brought to the West by the Dutch-Indonesian diaspora following independence.[17] However, many schools and systems tend to slip out of the public eye simply because they do not fit into the institution at opportunities shaped by the existing "pigeonholes" of martial arts community membership.

Not obviously part of the silat tradition, they often fail to find a place within the Nusantara martial arts communities, while they are often even more strictly excluded from the Totok context because of their reliance upon the indigenous Indo-Malay languages instead of any of the Chinese dialects.

How the Peranakanized systems synthesize the Nusantara and Chinese elements varies radically from school to school. Many seem to couple Chinese hand techniques to Nusantara ground-fighting skills drawn from arts like Harimau

Minangkabau and Pamacan with the sinuous body movements and agile footwork typical of silat. Similarly, many Peranakan kuntao systems shift their basic training away from long Chinese style "forms" to shorter combinations or exercises referred to in the Malay languages as *juru* or *jurus* (literally "skill"),[18] is and the adoption of musical performance with kendang and gamelan modeled on that used by silat. Another common trend is also the use of Nusantara weapons like the golok, parang, and *cabang* (also known as *siku-siku*; *trisula*; and *tekpi*, which is essentially a version of—and according to a number of authorities, the percursor to—the Okinawan sai) and so forth, rather than "classical" Chinese weapons.

The Peranakanization process necessarily appears to derive from two main pressures: a pressure to incorporate, or at least to counter, fighting skills and weapons indigenous to the Nusantara region (not to mention differences between the physical environments of southern China and Southeast Asia) on the one hand; and socio-cultural integration into Nusantara's traditions, kinaesthetic conventions, and public performance styles in the social context where training occurs.[19] The result is a range of culturally marginal arts that incorporate traits of both Chinese and Nusantara traditions and yet are quite distinct from the "orthodox" martial arts practiced in either.

Whither Kuntao?

It is apparent that when one speaks of "kuntao" one is not speaking of a single art, a single tradition, or even a single class or type of art. Rather, there exists a range of arts and systems scattered at various points along a trajectory of social and cultural integration ranged from the utterly orthodox Chinese systems virtually unchanged from their Mainland Chinese roots to completely integrated arts that have been fully absorbed within the bumiputra martial arts tradition, with many systems in a borderland having characteristics of both.

Roughly speaking, however, the various kuntao arts can probably be categorized according to the communities in which they occur. Some arts have lost or consciously abandoned a separate identity as kuntao arts, and define themselves as silat systems. At the other extreme, there are what might be termed Totok systems that consciously work at remaining as close to their Mainland Chinese heritage and practice as possible. However, there is also a very significant population of arts that exist in the interstices between the Chinese and the Nusantara; arts that represent a third, distinct tradition in their own right, which I have termed (after Suryadinata) "Peranakanized" systems.

The distinction drawn herein between Totok, Peranakan, and integrated systems is essentially an attempt to clarify an ambiguity in the notion of "kuntao" that occurs in the Nusantara use of the term. Intrinsically ambiguous, kuntao has found itself proscribed in and of itself along with the rest of the Nusantara Chinese marginal form. The alternative has been an intense pressure to abandon the marginal state, renounce one's Chinese heritage (whatever may be left of that for the Peranakan) and declare one's art to be silat, and politely overlook the sort of "obvious kuntao base" that commentators like Draeger find impossible to ignore.

More than simply a phenomenon of ambiguity and exclusion, the marginality of the Nusantara Chinese and their arts has a crucial temporal and transitional dimension to it. The danger of such a categorization, distinguishing between Totok, Peranakan, and integrated arts is that such a distinction is a synchronic one: a snapshot taken at a particular point in time or, rather, over a particular and relatively short period of time. Of the Indonesian Chinese, Leo Suryadinata concludes that: "... the younger generation of Totoks have rapidly become Indonesianized ... But are they being Indonesianized? Again, the answer depends on the geographical area and the social background of the individuals. It appears that the new generation Peranakans are being Indonesianized faster than Peranakanized Totoks. *If we draw a continuum, the Totok is being Peranakanized, while the Peranakan is being Indonesianized*" (Suryadinata, 1991: 19, emphasis added).

I have above used the term "trajectory" rather than "continuum" to describe the location of kuntao systems along the range from Totok through Peranakan to full integration for precisely this reason. It would appear that the location of arts along this continuum is really a series of snap-shots of a gradual, intergenerational movement towards complete integration in the Nusantara conventions of silat and pukulan.

This must necessarily prompt the question of the long-term survival of the many arts which bear the designation of "kuntao," particularly the distinctive, transitional, hybrid 'Peranakan' forms. The consequences of marginality can only have been exacerbated by decades of official antipathy. A number of authors writing on kuntao have remarked on a pervasive ban against kuntao in Indonesia, although the reasons for this prohibition have generally been melodramatic in the extreme. Bob Orlando has asserted of "kuntao's uncertain future" that the prohibition has arisen because "the practice of kuntao is discouraged in Indonesia because it is too violent . . . kuntaoers [sic] simply scare bureaucrats" (1996: 122–123). Draeger and Smith express the matter somewhat more moderately, stating that "Kun-tao is not for the masses. Apparently the Indonesian government thinks so too, for it has officially forbidden the classical study of kun-tao as detrimental to the political climate of the land" (1987: 184). The official edicts to which Draeger and Smith refer have been progressively attenuated or repealed in the last decade, while Orlando almost certainly overestimates the importance of kuntao for national policy-makers and civil servants.

Legal restraints aside, perhaps the most pervasive threat to the continued welfare of the Peranakanized kuntao systems is not faceless bureaucrats or nationalist governments, but simply the absence of an institutional role and position within the conceptual pigeonholes of the dominant, 'pure' martial arts communities. They have the choice between exile leading to extinction by starvation and normalization leading to extinction through absorption.

Just as kuntao practitioners are concerned about the ultimate survival of the art, Suryadinata asks "will the Ethnic Chinese survive" as a distinct population or, more accurately, two distinct populations? Suryadinata's conclusion is tentatively optimistic. In the first place, he points to "a revival of ethnicity around the world," although his suggestion, made at the height of the "Asian tiger boom" in 1991, before the currency crisis of the late 1990's, that ethnic particularism is likely to promote tolerance is less than compelling today. A more interesting suggestion is the notion that "the globalization of the Indonesian economy may also impede the Indonesianization process." Surydinata here appears to be suggesting that globalization attenuates artificial ethnic boundaries in preference for free trade (1991: 1920).

However, neither of these two possibilities holds much promise for the Peranakan kuntao systems. Self-conscious ethnic identity tends not to serve as a basis for cultural pluralism but instead for the abominations of "ethnic cleansing." It is more likely to increase intolerance of minorities and amplify integrationist tendencies than to reduce them.

On the other hand, globalization has proved no less pernicious with its emphasis on the marketable, high-profile and low-investment for quick payoff values of sport martial arts, and the increasingly uniform practice and training environment of "modern" techniques, "modern" ideas and "modern" values. All too often "globalization" means "Americanization," and so modernity has its own less formal, but perhaps far more pervasive integrationist pressures. If traditional systems with a clear-cut cultural and pedagogical identity have a hard time "selling" themselves in an age of Pay-per-view sporting martial arts, what hope have arts with a subtler and more uncertain identity?

If the Peranakanized kuntao systems are to survive as systems, it will have to be as a consequence of conscious attempts at preservation. Rather than trying to wedge these hybrid arts into the molds of either Chinese or Nusantara orthodoxy, there must be willful effort to assert their uniqueness and the benefits of learning from both traditions. One might almost imagine a variety of "Baperkism" for the Peranakanized martial arts. Much as the Peranakan Chinese may be seen as a Nusantara suku in their own right, so also perhaps the Peranakanized kuntao systems should be seen as a Nusantara aliran in their own right also. Some attempt at official acknowledgement might go a long way towards aiding the preservation process. If national regulatory bodies find it difficult to recognize Peranakanized kuntao systems within the silat canon, then perhaps a separate division for Peranakanized systems might be considered, distinct perhaps but ultimately more alike than differing.

Footnotes

1 This article is based on research undertaken on a combined ethnographic methodology. The informants included herein consist primarily of silat practitioners from the Singaporean Malay and Dutch-Indonesian emigre communities. However, it should be noted that although the Singaporean Nusantara peoples are legally classified as "Malay" for historical and political reasons, in fact approximately 80% of Singapore "Malays" are originally Indonesians who relocated to Singapore under the Japanese occupation as laborers, or fled to Singapore in the wake of the 1965 "generals' coup." Furthermore, as Lily Zubaidah Rahim has recently observed of the Singapore Malays: "The demographic cycles of the island's ancient history, from a population of several thousands in the era when it was a thriving trading port called Temasek in the eleventh century to only a thousand or so inhabitants in 1819, exemplifies the *atavistic merantau* (internal migration [for a detailed discussion of merantau, see Pauka, 1998: 81–83] tradition of Malay migration within the Nusantara . . . The Malay saying *Di mana bumi dipajak, di situlah langit dijunjong* ("on whatever soil we find ourselves, there we will hold up the sky") exemplifies the organic Singapore Malay identification with the Nusantara, of which Singapore is inextricably a part" (Rahim, 1998: 71).

The Singaporean informants were uniformly first or second-generation immigrants, many still with close family connections to Indonesia. The Dutch-Indonesians, or "Indos," interviewed were uniformly first generation emigres. A partial list of informants includes members of the Singapore Silat Community: Abdullah Shafiie Sidik (deputy president of Persekutuan Silat Singapure, PERSISI, of the originally Central Javanese system Cindai Puteh); Abdullah Zaini (Silat Jawa Banyuwangi); Awi Abulrahman (senior master of the Bugis Titi Pinang system); General Haji Ismaon (founding member of PERSISI); Jamaludin bin Malek (Kuntao Asli); Jamaludin Jamil (formerly secretary general of PERSISI, from Cekak Serantau); Mawardi Ifi (senior master of the Baweanese system Seligi Tunggal); Mohammad din Mohammad (Kuntao Melaka); Mohammed Khamin bin Said (from the Bugis art Titi Pinang, and formerly of Setia Hati Perhataman Tujuh Jurus, as well as a former secretary general of PERSISI); Mohammed Ramli Alwi (from the Bawean art Seligi Tunggal). Also Dutch-Indonesian emigres: David Liem (originally from Medan; Pukulan Cimande, various indigenous systems from Medan); Renee Scharff (originally from Semarang; Kuntao Macan, Silat Ambon); Richard Kudding (originally from Tanggerang, near Jakarta; Kuntao Macan, Pukulan) This was coupled with both direct observation of various schools and participant observation studying Titi Pinang under Mohohammad Khamin bin Said and Silat Jawa Banyuwangi under Abdullah Zaini. The author would like to thank PERSISI officials and members for their warm welcome and generous advice and assistance. Naturally, any error or misrepresentation herein is the responsibility of the author. I am grateful to Paatje Richard Kudding for instruction in a form of Indonesian kuntao that gave rise to the research in the article, and to Lee Wilson for his comments and advice on the first draft of this article.

2   "Nusantara" is an indigenous generic term for the entire linguistic and cultural community reaching from the ethnic Malays of southern Thailand in the west, north to Malaysia and east to Sulawesi, Kalimantan, Timor, Ambon, and (disputably) western Papua-New Guinea. Similarly, the indigenous generic for the peoples of Indonesia and Malaysia is *bumiputra*. The following discussion will argue that the problem of understanding kuntao as an art derives not from any exogenous conceptual difficulty of ethnographic description but, rather, an indigenous ambiguity of formulation. As a result, any understanding of the problem must follow Peter Winch's dictum of understanding people's actions in terms of their own frames of reference, and it will further be necessary to introduce and employ indigenous terms, concepts, and distinctions to effectively reconstruct the sociological dynamics at work.

3   This paper will employ the contemporary Romanization scheme for the Nusantara languages and dialects rather than the old Dutch-derived scheme, e.g. pukulan rather than poekoelan.

4   Constructing a reliable taxonomy of Nusantara combatives is a fraught task even at the best of times. The contemporary notion of 'pencak silat' is very much a product of the unifying and integrating efforts of post-independence organizations like IPSI (Ikatan Pencak Silat Indonesia) and PPSI (Persatuan Pencak Silat Indonesia), the terms *pencak* and *silat* originally being separate generic designations for Indo-Malay martial arts in different dialects (Sundanese and Sumatran Malay respectively), while Sundanese employs both *pencak* and *po* (Draeger, 1993: 42). The Minangkabau dialectal term is *silek* (Pauka, 1997,

18

1998). Many of the informants dealt with herein stressed a distinction between *pukulan* and *silat* in which silat is more 'artistic' and organized into schools (*perguruan*, lit. 'school or doctrine,' and *aliran*, lit. 'stream') and pukulan as being simpler, more utilitarian, characterized by personal and family systems. It is worth noting, however, that so-called pukulan systems were also reportedly confined the major coastal centers along the Java Sea, especially northern and northeastern Java (Jakarta, Semarang, Madura and the ethnic Maduranese in places like Bawean). Where silat is historically the war art of the *satria*, or warrior castes, pukulan was reportedly the art of sailors, fishermen and traders who picked up some good moves as they went around. However, even this description is complicated by the fact that the regions where pukulan is supposed to come from are also the areas in which the term pukulan turns up as a generic term for martial arts on a comparable linguistic footing to *silat*, *silek*, *pencak*, and *po*.

[5] The literal translation of *bumiputra* is "sons of the land," while *pribumi* simply means "of the land." It is worth pointing out that the bumiputra are not really the aboriginal peoples of the region. The aboriginals were typically of the Australasian ethnic family, and still survive in a somewhat marginalized status throughout the Nusantara as *orang asli* ("native people").

[6] The Nusantara languages are very agglomerative languages, a bit like Dutch or German. As a result, ideas are assembled from words and word roots coupled with a range of suffixes and prefixes. "Peranakan" employs the root *anak* ("child"), and in this case signifies that these ethnic Chinese are "children" of the Nusantara.

[7] It should be remembered that the pig is considered *haram*, or unclean, amongst the Muslim Malays.

[8] The twists and turns of realpolitik necessarily generate exceptions, but these are limitations upon the rule rather than a negation of it.

[9] *Suku* (from *suku bangsa*, "quarter-nation") meaning "ethnic group."

[10] *Pancasila* is the national ideology of Indonesia, and means "five principles," put briefly: 1) belief in one god, 2) a just and civilized humanity, 3) nationalism and unity, 4) democracy, and 5) social justice.

[11] So named after the Sukarno–era organization Baperki (the Consultative Body of Indonesian Citizenship) (Suryadinata, 1997: 8), although Suryadinata elsewhere traces the movement to the colonial era Partai Tionghua Indonesia (1981).

[12] Heavy-handed political control of official statistics and professional scholarship render Malaysian official figures amongst the least reliable in the nominally democratic world.

[13] The term "Indonesianized" is used here for convenience and to remain consistent

with Suryadinata's terminology. One might as well substitute "integrated," "normalized," or some neologism such as "Nusantaranized" that would surely be still more unwieldy than temporarily improvising around Suryadinata's "Indonesianization" notion.

14 In fairness to Draeger's groundbreaking efforts in the 1960's and the early 1970's, Mainland China was still behind closed borders and did not start to open up until the Canadian recognition of the Beijing government in 1972. As a result, the Overseas Chinese communities were the only primary source of information about Chinese martial arts. Authors of Draeger's generation tended to go into these communities with an eye toward the orthodox, and otherwise inaccessible, traditional Chinese martial arts. By the same token, Draeger's reportage frequently overlooks important indigenous conceptual and technical distinctions, not least that between pukulan and silat, especially in north-central and eastern Java.

15 I am indebted for the latter of these examples to the president of the UK Pencak Silat Federation, Aidinal Alrashid.

16 I am indebted to Abu Mansur, operator of the Pendakar world wide web site and the "gelanggang" mailing list for a first hand account of training in, and the structural characteristics of Kontan.

17 The following discussion will intentionally omit any detailed examination of the assortment of kuntao styles that were brought to the West by the emigre "Indo" communities. This is not because of any question of authenticity, but simply because the discussion developed here is intended to address a single case of cultural marginality. To incorporate "Indo" systems along with Nusantara-based systems would introduce an additional, and potentially cross-cutting ambiguity which would complicate the terms of analysis considerably, and well beyond the interests and requirements of the present discussion.

18 The spelling and use of the terms juru and jurus is also potentially a matter for contention among Western practitioners since the first generation gurus in the West were mainly Dutch-Indonesians who usually used the term *juru* rather than *jurus*. By way heading off a potential fracas over spelling, the various Nusantara languages underwent fairly extensive revision and some efforts at standardization in Malaysia, Indonesia, Singapore, and Brunei-Darusalam that resulted in the 1974 Romanization scheme, and some changes in vocabulary. So, for example, the Van Goort English-Indonesian dictionary written in the 1960's refers to the term *djuru* (*juru*) as "skill," while the more recent Oxford dictionaries of Bahasa Indonesia and Bahasa Malaysia employ the term jurus. Current IPSI/PERSILAT practice is to refer to *jurus* or *jurusan* which refer to "direction" rather than "skill." The derivation and use of either term in this context remains obscure. Note also

that the old Romanization scheme employed a Dutch-Germanic "j" (pronounced "y") and the dipthong "dj" to signify the English "j," but the new scheme employs the English "j." Similarly, the dipthong "tj" was replaced with a Pinyinesque "c."

[19] "Totok" Chinese systems have their own musical and dance performance traditions in the use of the large, single-headed drum, various cymbals and gongs to accompany forms performances, and the dance traditions of the lion and dragon dances. It is also interesting to note that silat performances and gongfu demonstrations and lion/dragon dances occur on analogous occasions, such as weddings, visits by community and political dignitaries, and the two cultures' respective New Year celebrations.

References

Dalton, B. (1989). *Indonesia handbook*. Chico, CA: Moon.

De Spa, H. (1997, July–December). Private correspondence.

Douglas, M. (1979). *Purity and danger: An analysis of concepts of pollution and taboo*. London: Routlege.

Draeger, D. (1993). *Weapons and fighting arts of Indonesia*. Rutland, VT: Charles Tuttle.

Draeger, D., & Smith, R. (1987). *Comprehensive Asian fighting arts*. New York: Kodansha.

Draeger, D., Tjoa, K., & Chambers, Q. (1983). *Shantung black tiger: A Shaolin fighting art of North China*. New York: Weatherhill.

Geertz, C. (1980). *Negara: The theatre state in nineteenth century Bali*. Princeton, NJ: Princeton University Press.

Haines, B. (1968). *Karate: It's history and traditions*. Rutland, VT: Charles Tuttle.

Kamarul A., Amiruddin. (1999, March). Perguruan seni silat kuntao 7. *Seni Beladiri*, No. 16, 13–15.

Lee, K. (1998). Singapore story: The memoirs of Lee Kuan Yew. Singapore: Times.

Mansur, A. (1998). Postings to the "gelanggang" mailing list. http://www.pendekar.com.

Maryono, O. (2000, February 18; download date). Kuntao in Indonesia. http://pendekar.com/oong/messages/48.html.

Orlando, B. (1996). *Indonesian fighting fundamentals: The brutal arts of the archipelago*. Boulder, CO: Paladin.

Othman, J. (1999, March). *Sao: Senjata utama Harimau Berantai*. Seni Beladiri, No. 16, 50–52.

Pauka, K. (1997). Silek: The martial arts of West Sumatra. *Journal of Asian Martial Arts*, 6(1), 62–79.

Pauka, K. (1998). *Theatre and martial arts in West Sumatra*. Athens, OH: Ohio

University Press.

Rahim, L. (1998). *The Singapore dilemma: The political and educational marginality of the Malay community*. Oxford, England: Oxford University Press.

Rashid, R. (1990). Martial arts and superman. In Wazir Jahan Karim (Ed.), *Emotions of culture: A Malay perspective*. Singapore: Oxford University Press.

Sheppard, M. (1983). *Taman Saujana: Dance, drama, music and magic in Malaysia long and not-so-long ago*. Petaling Jaya, Malaysia: International Book Service.

Suryadinata, L. (1981). *Peranakan Chinese politics in Java 1917–1942*. Singapore: Singapore University Press.

Suryadinata, L. (1997). *The culture of the Chinese minority in Indonesia*. Singapore: Times.

Weber, M. (1982). *General economic history*. London: Transaction.

Chasing the Magic:
Mysticism and the Martial Arts
on the Island of Java

by James Wilson, J.D., Dip. Ac./Lic. Ac.

Borobudur. Courtesy of Rumah Dharma, Flicker.

Of all Asian martial arts, pencak silat is perhaps the least well known beyond the borders of its own native Indonesia. Even experienced martial artists in the U.S. often possess little more than a passing familiarity with this fascinating art form. For centuries its secrets have remained carefully guarded by both hermetic masters and practitioners of the royal courts. Even in the days of a democratic republic, Indonesia has until only recently maintained pencak silat as a national treasure not for export, largely due to the role guerrilla bands of unarmed martial artists played in the fight for independence against the Dutch following World War II. Their successes are largely believed to be the result of pencak silat's peculiar mystical practices and manipulation of *tenaga dalam*, or inner force, a variant of qi with a uniquely Indonesian twist. Though there have recently been a few articles in English that discuss of pencak silat's physical techniques, the style's other elements still remain but a shadowy mystery beyond the waters of this archipelagic nation. Understanding these elements is integral to understanding the true meaning of pencak silat and its pivotal role in Indonesian history and popular folk belief.

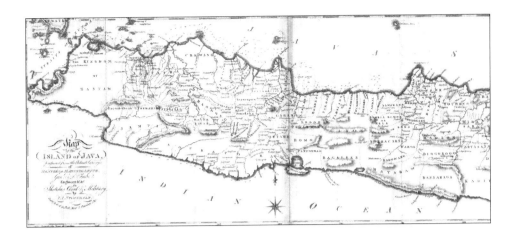

1812 Map of Java, Indonesia.
Courtesy of British Library HMNTS 010055.e.4.

The words *pencak* and *silat* both imply a system of self-defense or fencing. Most scholars, however, believe silat to be pencak's martial application. Pencak itself, as expressed through dance forms often accompanied by music, reflects the style's aesthetic nature and serves a function similar to the role of kata in Japanese karatedo. These two are not identical, however. In daily language Indonesians frequently abbreviate pencak silat to merely silat. The practice or use of self-defense is referred to as *bersilat* (*ber* meaning to have, to possess, i.e., to possess silat). The term silat is often used in reference to other Asian fighting forms, such as taekwondo and karate, yet the term pencak never stands alone and is never utilized in the description or definition of fighting styles not indigenous to Indonesia. While silat may be found around the globe, pencak silat is a uniquely Indonesian phenomenon.

Here language betrays the Indonesian perception of a distinct difference between pencak silat and all other martial arts. This is not simply a difference in physical technique (*silat*) alone. The main difference lies in the presence of pencak, which goes beyond the merely aesthetic to encompass everything outside the style's physical realm, namely its spiritual and even mystical elements. These qualities have historically enjoyed a symbiotic relationship with the various religious traditions that have played a role in the evolution of Indonesian consciousness and cosmology.[1] As Indonesia in some respects may be viewed as a religious state,[2] understanding what pencak silat has given to and borrowed from the nation's spiritual heritage is integral to understanding all aspects of contemporary Indonesian society. No aspect of modern Indonesia, from personal life to the realm of politics and economics, can be properly understood without reference to these forces. The island of Java, which

24

possesses 70% of the nation's 190 million people and is historically the home of the archipelago's great empires prior to the arrival of Dutch colonists at the outset of the seventeenth century, will be the focus of this study. The royal courts of these Javanese god-kings were the crucible in which pencak silat is claimed to have been refined to its present technical and spiritual embodiment.

Theories on the Origin of Pencak Silat

Pencak silat is actually believed to have originated on neighboring Sumatra, the easternmost of Indonesia's five main islands. Some credit the style's creation to monks of the Mahayana Buddhist Sriwijaya Empire (seventh to twelfth century CE), centered around the southern Sumatran seaport of Palembang. The monks were said to have derived their fighting techniques from the close observation of animals, though a more folkloric treatment acknowledges pencak silat as a peasant creation. The story tells of a West Sumatran village woman who was sent by her husband to gather water. Near the water well she was distracted from her task by a battle between a bird and a snake. The bird was unable to fly away because of a wounded wing and, being no match for the cunning serpent, could do nothing but fend off the snake's advances. Eventually the snake became so weary from his incessant attacking, however, that the bird was able to take the offensive and vanquish his fatigued foe. Satisfied, the woman fetched her water and returned home, unaware of how long she'd been gone. Her husband, furious at her tardiness, went to beat her. Imagine his surprise when, remembering the bird's tactics, his wife was likewise able to fend off his attacks and eventually subdue him! Thus was pencak silat born.

The true progenitor of pencak silat may be found in the synthesis of these two explanations. Palembang was an important seaport bringing trade from across the Orient. Buddhist missionaries from both India and China frequented the capital of the Sriwijaya Empire, undoubtedly bringing their own martial techniques with them. Pencak silat possesses some similarities to Indian grappling techniques, while the wushu of China's Shaolin temples contain many styles derived from animal fighting forms (i.e., Eagle Claw, White Crane, Praying Mantis, Monkey and Tiger). The foundation for these forms is said to have been laid down in the *Yi Jin Jing* text of Damo, who himself was of Indian descent, and a Buddhist Prince of the Chinese Liang dynasty just one century prior to the rise of the Sriwijaya in Indonesia. The story of wushu's creation along with many of its techniques may have been adopted by the early practitioners of pencak silat. A piece of creative mythology such as our second story crediting pencak silat's development to a woman[3] may betray the contributions made to the style by the West Sumatran Minangkabau, a matriarchal tribe whose martial style possesses characteristic traits found dispersed throughout the islands of the archipelago. While Buddhist monks may have brought martial arts to Indonesia, these forms did not remain there unchanged. As the closest kingdom geographically to the Sriwijaya, the Minangkabau undoubtedly usurped some of wushu's secrets. These were then adapted or elaborated upon, such changes bearing a uniquely Indonesian flavor.

One such distinction is the much closer resemblance of pencak silat styles to the animal it tries to emulate. Tiger silat, for example, is fought close to the ground, the practitioner stalking, crawling and springing from all fours, belly parallel to the earth. Monkey styles are performed in a low crouch with arms loose, often flailing for slaps and grabs, the knuckles nearly dragging on the ground prior to closing in for the attack. It is from this style that *depok* and *sempok* are derived. These deep crouch and squatting postures serve as fundamental stances in many pencak silat styles and, along with *harimau* (tiger) silat, create a repertoire of techniques unlike any other in the martial world. They are simultaneously intimidating, yet more primitive, as the martial artist seemingly becomes the animal characteristic of the style.

Sometimes the artist actually does take on the animal characteristic, as may be seen in the fine line between silat and *ilmu*, which is alternately translated as science or esoteric knowledge. The one who employs ilmu doesn't simply emulate a given animal, but, through trance, becomes possessed by the spirit of the summoned beast. The possessed individual claims no awareness of anything that occurs during the time of his possession, which will last until the exorcism of the spirit by some more powerful entity or the elimination of whatever threat gave necessity to its being channelled. My friend Darnato, who hails from a small village in the vicinity of Borobudur temple in Central Java, "practices" *ilmu kera*, the science of the monkey. He calls upon the monkey's spirit with his own mind while simultaneously creating a self-induced trance through a quick series of breathing techniques. From that point on his actions are not premeditated, but are the instinctual responses of a primate. Because he is no longer guided by his own mind, but by that of a spirit, his physical body faces many of the same limitations placed on spirits according to both Javanese and silat tradition. One such limitation is that he cannot cross a line drawn by a higher spiritual adept using their tenaga dalam.[4] Such restrictions are not unusual. Most styles of pencak silat which utilize ilmu in the form of mantras[5] and possession carry some sort of limitation or side-effect with their use. One form of *ilmu ular* (snake) which may be learned in the hills of Banten, West Java, enables the practitioner to spit venomous saliva from the ducts beneath his tongue like a cobra, or so I've been told. Each time this is done, however, the individual's complexion grows darker, which is considered an undesirable physical trait in modern Indonesia due to its perceived relationship with unskilled manual labor. Ilmu, though related, is not the same as tenaga dulam.

Ilmu is not taught in any pencak silat styles under the umbrella of Ikatan Pencak Silat of Indonesia (IPSI). The continued presence of ilmu and tenaga dalam in Indonesia is important, however, if one is to understand where the bridge between pencak silat's physical technique and mystical practice was first crossed. Such an understanding first requires an examination of Java's religious legacy.

The Influence of Animism

Prior to the arrival of Buddhism and Hinduism in Indonesia around the fourth century CE, animism was the major vehicle of faith and continues to manifest itself in various ways throughout the islands. One example from Western Java is *kuda lumping*. Kuda is Indonesian for "horse," while kuda lumping may be translated as "the horse dance" or "leaping horse." A means of entertainment as well as spiritual release, children and adults alike gather to watch the village men ride upon horses mad of bamboo and woven rattan. The dance is performed to the accompaniment of a few instruments taken from the *gamelan* orchestra, gamelan being the traditional music most characteristic of Java. It is predominantly a percussive ensemble using a variety of metallophones. The instruments used in kuda lumping are the *kendang*, a traditional *dru*, one or two gongs of hammered bronze, and a wooden flute called the *suling*. The suling weaves a tapestry of melody and harmony that serves to entice and ensnare the willing soul, leading his mind into trance which is then maintained by the steady drone of the resonating gongs. The kendang's rhythmic pounding waxes and wanes in volume and intensity throughout the performance but becomes the predominant instrument at the finale, beckoning the dancers back to this world from the land of spirits.

The name of this dance does not come from the garishly decorated rattan hobby horses, however. These are merely reflections of the dance's true source, the horse spirits that descend upon the dancers and occupy their souls. Sometimes other spirits will come also, who may give advice to the village or prophesy events for the coming year. The arrival of such spirits is often accompanied by acts commonly known as *debus*, a form of self-mutilation. Amongst the Vodoun of Haiti a similar dance takes place, in which human hosts hold hot coals upon their tongues while riding horse spirits that have descended from the heavenly realms.

What is this life flowing in our bodies like fire? What is it?

—*The Mahabharata*

27

Carried away by trance, a dancer recoils before the lash of the whip during a Dayakan performance.

A similar dance may be found in the villages of Central Java near the temple of Borobudur. Called *Dayakan*, it is believed to have been brought to the area by the Dayak of Kalimantan, an island to the north of Java. The Dayak are known more romantically in the West as the wild men, or head hunters, of Borneo. The performance's participants wear helmet-like masks characterizing various animals in the hope that the spirit of some such beast will possess them during the dance. While watching, I myself could feel the lure to enter the trance, which I fought by becoming preoccupied with my camera. One spectator, a young villager, whose acquaintance I had made previously, proved unable to distract his mind from the enticing music and exploded upon the dance with such fury he knocked one dancer prostrate on the ground. It took three grown men and a *dukun* (shaman),[6] who lashed him repeatedly with a bull whip to bring him under control.

He was not the only one from the audience to fall under the intoxicating spell of the suling, either. While in the throes of trance, all participants fought, stampeded and fended off attack like various beasts, reacting to the dukun's whip as would any creature of the wild. Many of their body contortions intimated pencak silat maneuvers. Undoubtedly the styles of ilmu such as *kera, harimau,* and *ular* evolved from such dances centuries ago, when Buddhist missionaries unwittingly disseminated amongst an animist peasantry the fundamental elements of their martial arts along with their metaphysics. Another vestige of animistic ritual in pencak silat is the presence of *gumelan*, as it is used by Kuda Lumping or Dayakan, in the practice of *senam*. Senam, or gymnastics, is to pencak silat what the kata is to karatedo. What is unique, however, is that the routines are choreographed to music.

While pencak silat is fierce, senam's predecessor, due to the presence of ilmu, is a much more frightening affair to observe. Once the trance had begun there were no smiles, no laughing, just blank, amazed and confused expressions. The animals, for that is what they had become, were given an offering of food. This was mostly grasses and fodder, though it is often mixed with ground glass to prove the validity of their possession. They ate ravenously, their faces in the earth like snouts and muzzles. It is imperative that the offering be complete and each animal eat its fill. Unsatisfied spirits have been known to keep their human hosts, who then never returned from their state of possession. The tigers are usually the last to go, even mauling the drummer as he calls the spirit out of the man. Once the demon has been exorcised the dancer collapses and is carried away. He will remain unconscious for anywhere from five to fifteen minutes. Upon revival there is little recollection. I spoke with a few individuals after their journey through the spirit world. They stated that during the trance everything seemed far away, and there was no good or bad, no thought. Everything was part of their existence. They acted and reacted as seemed appropriate, natural, instinctive.

From its 122 square meter base, Borobudur's 3,000 relief sculptures decorate five galleries that rise up to form a giant mandala. These sculptures serve to educate those who walk among them about the life and teachings of Gautama Buddha, whose birth, death, and enlightenment are commemorated by thousands of pilgrims from around the world every May during the ceremony of Waicak.

Hindu and Buddhist Influences

Thus animism, as the first major player on the Javanese religious scene, has been demonstrated to be the initial source of pencak silat's mystical tradition. The second major factor is Hinduism. Java's first Hindu dynasty, the Sanjaya, rose to power almost simultaneously with the appearance of the Sriwijaya in Sumatra. Javanese shamanism and animism, already familiar with meditation, trance and other altered states of consciousness, quickly made Hindu yoga practices their own. Though frequently incomplete or inexact and often not fully understood by their practitioners, these practices may still be observed in pencak silat today. As we will discuss later, through breath control techniques, much of tenaga dalam (tenaga meaning force, dalam meaning inner) is generated at the various chakras, centers along the human anatomy that have proven auspicious for the collection of what is now known to Western science as bioelectricity.[7] In Kundalini Yoga this energy, known as prana, is said to emanate from the body's source of sexual energy. From here it is refined as it ascends through the various chakra to the enlightened centers of mind and spirit at the crown of the head. This process, often illustrated by two serpents intertwined along the central axis of the spinal column, is designed to nourish the brain and eventually bring spiritual enlightenment. While tenaga dalam has its own spiritual roots and purposes, it manifests itself in a much more immediate fashion that enters the realm of superheroics, with obvious martial applications. To understand the origin of these astounding abilities we must first explore the Hindu concept of dharma.

Dharma is a Sanskrit word denoting the divine order that supports the universe. Originally derived from the order of the observed zodiac, the cyclical manifestation of heavenly bodies upon which the functions of hunting, navigation, agriculture and civilization's early city states were founded, dharma was at one time the expression of cosmic order in the lives of men. This order constituted a submission by the individual to his role in the play of life, which succeeded in taming the nomad of the plains so as to create a predictable society, a society so predictable it could practically organize and govern itself. Such a self-perpetuating system was crucial for the first enterprising efforts at creating a civilization, the caretaker of which had no previous models to follow. The self-actualization of trance, vision and possession inherent in shamanistic and animistic tradition was thereby tethered, man's animal spirit being put on an astrological leash whereby individual behavior was constricted by a title, the parameters of which were as constant as the stars. The various roles of society were fulfilled by keeping the masses in a right relationship with the cosmos through delineations of caste. A person did not exist as an individual, but as a priest, a warrior, a merchant, or an untouchable. Distinction of caste was hereditary, as unchangeable as the stars above, and would guide every function of an individual's life from birth to death: his home, his religion, his schooling, employment, marriage, associations; even one's clothing and diet. The betterment of one's lot was to be accomplished not for this life, but the next, through an adherence to caste restrictions. Failure to do so procured divine punishment. This was not the judgment of a fickle, personal God like that of Christianity or Islam, but the automatic action of the divine principle of order woven through the fabric of the universe. This is dharma.

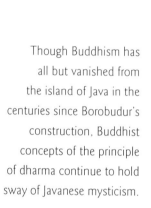

Though Buddhism has all but vanished from the island of Java in the centuries since Borobudur's construction, Buddhist concepts of the principle of dharma continue to hold sway of Javanese mysticism.

It is easy to see, in light of our previous glimpse of Javanese animism, why folklore characterizes the introduction of Hinduism to Java as the arrival of art, culture and civilization to soothe the savage beast. Supposedly when the gods looked down from the heavens they were unable to tolerate the island's barbaric ways. They plucked the twin of Mount Meru from its home in the Himalayas and placed the holy mountain on Java in an attempt to bring order to the island's chaotic ferocity. This, according to legend, is Mount Semeru, the tallest of Indonesia's over sixty active volcanoes. Despite the tumultuous lava deep within its cauldron's steaming maw, Semeru's rich volcanic ash helps make Java's plains among the most fertile in the world. Lush, green, tropical foliage gives testimony to the life-giving properties of Java's cosmic mountain, symbol of dharma. Dharma has its most perfect representation in the man-made mountain of Borobudur, however, the largest Buddhist temple in the world. During Buddhism's brief period of dominance in Central Java, the religion made a distinctive impression on the island's mysticism. We've already seen how its presence on Sumatra may well have introduced martial arts to the Indonesian archipelago. What we're concerned with now is how Buddhist belief transformed the Hindu concept of dharma. These changes had massive repercussions on the mystical practices of pencak silat.

In Buddhism, dharma became a rather ambiguous term. Definitions ranged from the One Ultimate Reality, which is similar to its original meaning, to being any quality, thing, or even state of mind. Dharma remained, for most mortal men, the divine fate determining the steps of their lives from birth until death and into which they caught but brief glimpses. Those who attained Buddhist enlightenment transcended dharma in this sense, however, as Buddhist teaching allowed them to correctly perceive the things, qualities and mental states that constitute the One Ultimate Reality behind this world of illusion. The enlightened thereby obtained mastery over the seen and unseen world through their intimate knowledge and unity therewith. For the one, dharma controls. For the other, dharma is control. Though Buddhism has all but vanished from Java in the millennium following Borobudur's construction, this control continues to be the aim of traditional practitioners of Javanese mysticism. The Buddhist text, *Patisambhidu*, credits those who have achieved a degree of intimacy with the dharma with the ability to project their image or even duplicate themselves a thousand times. They are capable of passing through solid matter, of diving into and out of the earth as if it were water, and of walking on water as if it were earth. Levitation, even flight is not impossible, though instantaneous transportation by power of thought is more expedient. For the mischievous at heart, invisibility is worth a try. This new magic superseded the ilmu of animist Java. No longer was a human being merely possessed by an animal spirit, but the human spirit became capable of transforming its own flesh and blood into that of a bird, dragon, or even a god! Thus we see how dharma entered into the wild territories of Javanese shamanism and tamed the animistic beast, providing a sense of cosmic order, the unknown plan of the gods that determine our every step. But it simultaneously provided the means by which to attain a magic and freedom far greater than any the savage beast had to offer.

It is interesting to note that the members of the only Hindu-Buddhist community still extant on the island today, the Tenggerese of East Java, do not believe in any of these forms of ilmu. Living on a high plateau in the shadow of Semeru, the Tenggerese are adamant in stating the difference between the dukun characteristic of Central Java and the priests that promulgate their own Hindu-Buddhist faith. Their ceremony, liturgy and trance are simply a means to remain cohesive as a people by commemorating their ancestors and constantly recreating the Tengger creation myths. These acts also secure good fortune for the future. While such aspects of fidelity, a manifestation of dharma in its original sense, are integral to the martial arts brotherhoods of contemporary pencak silat, no distinct mode of self-defense is known to have originated within the Tengger, much less any form of ilmu. As the Tenggerese are believed to be the island's sole remaining caretakers of pre-Islamic Javanese faith, it would seem that the arrival of Hinduism and Buddhism in Indonesia merely provided the mystical and metaphysical ground-work for something not yet cemented into the Javanese mindset until the island's overwhelming conversion to Islam during the fifteenth and sixteenth centuries CE. By what manner could the strict legalism and monotheism of Islam be made to accommodate the tenets of another faith? This is especially bewildering when these tenets are not really an established doctrine, but the exciting, dynamic, intermingling aromas of a potpourri, a smorgasbord of faiths aimed not at submission to a divine will, but to human enlightenment through the liberation of an individual's inner soul.[8]

To understand this apparent enigma it is important to point out that all major religions of influence on Java arrived approximately one thousand years after conception in their land of origin, which is more than ample time for a faith to evolve, be canonized, and fall into apostasy. As Indonesia was never really occupied by a hostile foreign element prior to the Dutch arriving at the start of the seventeenth century, the various competing sects of a religion were generally brought to the archipelago by traders or missionaries with whom good relations were cultivated or by members of their own kingdoms who had traveled to distant lands.[9] Also, although some religions evolved from preceding faiths in the countries in which they were founded, these faiths may have arrived simultaneously in Java. While Hinduism had already been in evolution for nearly 1500 years in India prior to the birth of Gautama Buddha in 563 BCE, neither of these religions came to Java until approximately 400 CE. The Hindu-Buddhist tradition in Java didn't enjoy two millennia of evolutionary history as it did in India. The Hindu Sanjaya and Buddhist Sailendra dynasties were consolidating their kingdoms on the island less than three centuries after their respective faiths had washed up on Java's shores. This may be enough time to build temples, even an empire, but it is woefully insufficient for displacing an animist tradition that reaches back into prehistory. Furthermore, as various political entities fought for control over Java's fertile, arable lowland plans, it was common practice for the subjugated kingdom to be forced to adopt the faith of its conquerors. In an attempt to preserve its original heritage within that of a conquering culture, a religion's proponents would often teach its populace that the two faiths were synonymous.[10] One can therefore see why various traditions were then syncretized, rather than becoming merely successive. This syncretic attitude remains intact to the present day. The One True God, *Ketuhanan Yang Maha Esa*, in which all Indonesians must believe according to the nation's guiding doctrine of Pancasila,[2] is not identified by the Indonesian word Tuhan, meaning God, but by the word Ketuhanan. The affixes ke- and -an denote more of a "concept" of divinity. The resulting deity remains singular and supreme, Maha

Esa, yet indifferentiated, and thereby able to encompass the great diversity of beliefs that have contributed to Indonesian culture. This is evident by the fact that, despite its status as the world's largest Muslim nation, Indonesia's national emblem is the *garuda*, the mythological bird that brought the elixir of the gods to humanity in the Hindu *Mahabharata* epic. The elixir the garuda bears upon modern Indonesia's emblem is the nation's motto, *Bhinneka Tunggal Ika*, which means "unity in diversity," an example of syncretism in action.

Java's Historical Development and Syncretic Outlook

Thus we see two major trends: one, the tendency for a religion to fall into apostasy over time; the second, a result of Java being a center of international trade and shipping, namely, the constant influx of new and competing faiths to the island. The combination of these trends enabled the Javanese to accept Islam while perpetuating previous religious traditions that have proven, under normal circumstances, to be mutually exclusive. The assimilation of many layers of belief, the necessity of their harmonization for the purpose of preventing cultural and ethnic clashes, and when such clashes do occur, the re-establishment of harmony as a means of cultural preservation for the subjugated entity, all worked together to build a unique coping mechanism within Javanese psychology. *Basabasi* is referred to throughout the archipelago as the single most distinguishing trait of Javanese culture. Literally translated as "beating around the bush," basabasi has a few distinct characteristics, namely the playing down of differences and the reluctance to state anything negative.

The creative mythology inherent in such an outlook on life explains why the implied magic within Java's strange amalgam of faiths failed to manifest itself in Tenggerese society, instead waiting for the rise of Central Java's first Islamic kingdom, the greatest challenge to Javanese principles of acceptance and harmonization, to be forged into the mystic practices we see today. The initial rulers of this kingdom, the empire of Mataram, actually subscribed to the Hindu faith of the preceding Majapahit Dynasty, from whose customs were drawn the five principles of Pancasila. As the Majapahit Empire began to crumble at the end of the fifteenth century, Islam made inroads into Indonesia's coastal territories through Arabic traders. In the power vacuum following the Majapahit's demise, there were constant attempts by these small coastal kingdoms to expand their territories into the rice bowl of Central Java that forced the land owning peasantry of Mataram to unite. Their first ruler, Panembahan Krapyak (r. 1601–1613), found his reign to be constantly plagued by these kingdoms' advances.

Mataram's second leader, Raden Mas Rangsang, who ascended the throne under the Hindu title Prabu Pandita, or King-Priest, immediately began to orchestrate his own version of reality to alleviate the dilemmas faced by his predecessor. First his court scribe created a fictional predecessor to Krapyak by the name of Senapati.[11]

Senapati (r. 1550–1600), was credited with many royal marriages during the time of his fictional rule which simultaneously established Rangsang's royal descent while creating familial bonds by which to forge treaties with neighboring kingdoms. When Rangsang chose to break those treaties he used the same familial bonds to stake a claim to their thrones. As he succeeded in taking these thrones by military conquest, his fictional heritage was supported rather than challenged by his opponents, as it is far more honorable to have been conquered by royalty than peasant serfs.

In territories where political as well as religious allegiances were afforded Islamic *ulanzas* and *walis*,[12] Rangsang had himself crowned with the Muslim title of *Susuhunan*. He then went on to slaughter dissenting religious leaders, leaving himself as the sole object of the people's devotion. The new Susuhunan's title was used by the people as evidence of his Islamic faith in order to justify his right to rule by divine providence, thereby excusing their inability to deny him the throne. As a further demonstration of his divine mandate, legends began to arise stating he journeyed thousands of kilometers to pray at Mecca every Friday by power of his magic, or ilmu. The Susuhunan's court undertook the creation of an entirely new language, Bahasa Jawa, with three speech levels to accentuate who was who in Javanese society or, more specifically, who was king.[13] Bahasa Jawa spread extensively within a century and remains the daily language of contemporary Central and Eastern Java.

At this time the Susuhunan bestowed upon himself a new Islamic title, that of Sultan, to accompany his new name of *Agung*. Agung means "great," or "grand" and alludes to the well known concept among the Javanese of *keagung-binataraan*, meaning "celestial grandeur." The secondary root, *binatara*, is derived from *batara*, or "god," and is itself defined as "glorified god." Sultan Agung's near divine stature credited him with all the abilities similarly offered previous kings through Buddhist means. With Sultan Agung came the first chronicling of the powers of *kekuatan, ilmu,* and *tenaga dalam* that make pencak silat a uniquely Indonesian phenomenon.[14]

How could Islam, a religion of submission, tolerate a Sultan who elevated himself to the realm of divinity? As stated previously, the reign of Sultan Agung (r. 1613–1645), during which Islam solidified its presence and the form in which it would manifest itself on Java to the present day, did not occur until one thousand years after the religion's birth in the Middle East. Like all faiths, this time had allowed Islam to experience such apostasy as to produce many sects, some of which did not even remotely resemble the teachings of Mohammed himself. It was just such a sect that now came to the fore in Java.

Sufism, Islam's mystical sect, originated around the beginning of the twelfth century CE. It is, however, a product of Greek thought stemming from the fourth century BCE. The philosophies of Plato, brought to India through the conquests of Alexander, made an incredible impression on Hindu-Buddhist thinking. The Platonic Ideal, run through the filter of Hindu dharma, then made its way back to the Mediterranean, where Buddhist missionaries had reached as far as Egypt by the time of Christ. Here they may have served to influence hermetic communities such as the Essenes, evidence of which may be seen by the overtones of Eastern thought in New Testament writings. By the fifth century CE, Manichaeism, a synthesis of Buddhist, Zoroastrian and Christian philosophies, had spread from its Persian beginnings to reach as far as Africa and China. Over the next seven centuries, this continued growth in Eastern influence over Mediterranean religions had become so strong that in the late twelfth and early thirteenth century writings of the great Sufi thinker Ibn' Arabi, the stories of the Judeo-Christian-Islamic tradition, as presented by the *Koran*, had become merely vessels for an ontology and metaphysics derived almost entirely from a synthesis of Platonic and Hindu-Buddhist ideas.[15]

While Sufism always remained a minor movement in Islam's homeland of the Middle East, it became a major force in Indonesia. Conversion did not constitute a change, but merely an addition to one's current faith of another name for God (Allah), another prophet (Mohammed), and a new source of legend (the Koran). All other aspects of Sufism bore far greater resemblance to pre-existing Javanese beliefs than the standard interpretation of Mohammed's teachings. To this day, some Islamic adherents do not even accept Sufis as being Muslim. When almost one thousand Indonesians died of suffocation and heat exhaustion in a traffic tunnel during the Haji to Mecca in 1990, there were those who stated it was an act of Allah condemning their heresy.

In Sufism God is worshiped, not as the all powerful Allah, but as an abstract force, similar to dharma, which may manifest itself in many different ways, as consistent with animism and the Hindu pantheon of gods. In fact, the worship of a well defined omnipotent creator without accompanying forms of idolatry is explicitly condemned.[16] Sufi belief proposes two types of enlightenment. *Haqua'iq* is synonymous with Buddhist enlightenment and contains all the magical powers inherent in one who has obtained unity with and control over *tanzih*, the Sufi equivalent of dharma as the divine cosmic order. What is unique to Sufism is the emphasis that this state of spirituality must be preceded by another, "minor" enlightenment known as *kashf*. While haqua'iq is primarily based on knowledge, kashf is an immediate experience of God, or Dharmu, in all its manifest forms, called *tashbih*. This experience cannot be described with words nor grasped by ordinary reason; all that exists for someone who has had this experience is natural desire and instinct.[17] This is nearly the exact description of trance I had received from the participants of Kuda Lumping, Dayakan, and pencak silat's various forms of ilmu concerning animal possession. Indeed, Ibn' Arabi stated that any man, upon attainment of this first enlightenment, became an animal, pure and simple.[18] Those who attain Arabi's second enlightenment realize that they are part of God and thereby obtain god-like powers. Thus, had Java found a faith, or had a faith found Java? Mohammed, as interpreted by Sufism, was the last true prophet of God, and his message was that shamanistic practices, when undertaken with Hindu asceticism, yield Buddhist enlightenment. This metaphysical formula, combined with the creative mythology inherent in the Javanese sociological phenomenon of basabasi, was the fertile soil in which the seeds of pencak silat's mysticism came to full bloom. This may be illustrated by the *wayang kulit*, the shadow puppet plays characteristic of Central Java.

It may seem ironic that the wayang kulit came into prominence during the Islamic Mataram's founding, since the source of the art form's most revered legends are the Hindu *Mahabharata* and *Ramayana* epics. On second examination, however, it becomes apparent that there is no mystery about this occurrence. It is also no coincidence that many *dalangs*, or puppeteers, are both powerful mystics and skilled practitioners of pencak silat.[19] While the manipulation of the puppets does require the same strong hands and deft finger movements necessary for good silat technique, there are much more evident reasons for this strength. One is the incredible physical discipline dalangs must possess. A dalang will typically fast the day of a performance and cannot eat until a show concludes at sunrise, as such plays last all night. He will not move from his cross-legged position before the screen during the performance's full nine hours. From there he will conduct the orchestra behind him, play percussive accents with a wood block wedged between his toes, tell jokes, sing, preach and teach, while manipulating each of up to three hundred puppets himself and providing all of their voices. His physical discipline goes beyond that of an athlete to become ascetic denial, enhancing his role as a mystic. Also, the entire symbolism inherent in a wayang performance is a summation of Sufi metaphysics, a living representation of Javanese philosophy and cosmology.[20]

But the final reason for wayang kulit's popularity in Islamic Java and its close relationship with pencak silat is the Hindu legends it recreates. Told for the purpose of educating the largely illiterate populace of seventeenth century Java with regard to centuries of religious tradition, the heroes of the wayang kulit served as virtuous role models for those aspiring to the powers of enlightenment discussed previously. Within the *kratons*, or palaces, of Yogyakarta and Surakarta in Central Java, there arose among the aristocracy groups of men who called themselves the satria, after the Hindu warrior caste from which these heroes sprang. Often minor ministers of protocol within the Sultan's court, these men would try to emulate the legendary figures of the *wayang kulit*, who were a combination of errant knight and religious ascetic. The satria would practice their martial skills and weapons dexterity, but would also go into self-imposed exile in caves along the coast or in mountain hermitages for the purposes of meditation[21] and fasting.[22] Individual members of the satria would often congregate and form brotherhoods centered around a single hero from the wayang kulit.

One such character is Bima from the *Mahabharata*. The son of Dewi Kunti, Bima was born with a thick, impenetrable afterbirth in which his newborn body was still encased. Seen as a potential evil omen, his mother cast him away into the forest. For members of the pencak silat style known as Bima Sakti, these humble beginnings serve as an illustration of *rendah hati*, the humble heart.

Ravaged by time and the area's incredible seismic activity, the ruins of Dieng plateau are but remnants of a vast Hindu temple complex of the seventh century CE. One of the best preserved temples is that of Bima, upon whose character the pencak silat school of Bima Sakti is based.

Abandoned in the forest, the infant Bima was attacked by an elephant. However, with each attempt by the elephant to rip his birth sac open, Bima grew in strength and stature, and when he finally emerged from his encasement he had grown strong enough to subdue his attacker. From this story the martial artist is taught that it is better to be the first struck than the first to strike. Because of his or her tenaga dalam, an adept practitioner of pencak silat is said to be capable of bruising or breaking the limbs of an opponent simply through passive blocking.[23]

Only as a last resort does a member of Bima Sakti employ violence himself, but at that time it is for the complete neutralization of the enemy, even if it means the enemy's death. It is no wonder that, though Bima Sakti is a member of IPSI, it along with six other schools which employ tenaga dalam, is not allowed to compete in sparring competition with any other martial forms. Individuals under eighteen years old are required to present written permission from their parents to study, and all members must leave a copy of their citizenship card on registration with the local police, who in turn must supply the instructor with a letter stating the applicant has no prior criminal record and is studying the martial art with good intent. This good intent is seen as synonymous with the chivalrous character of Bima.

Bima, having been 'hatched,' as it were, was later returned to his family. In the uniquely Javanese version of this Indian myth, Bima is the uniting force of five brothers. In this way Bima symbolizes Java, which unites the five main islands of Indonesia.[24] He also represents Ketuhanun Yang Mahu Esa, the first of Pancasila's five principles, the latter four of which are only deemed possible because of the first.[25] The upholding of these five principles largely constitute the moral obligation of Bima Sakti's members.[26] This obligation is emphasized by the use and practice of *lima pokok*, the five staple strikes learned by all beginning students. The mutual goal of Bima Sakti and Pancasila is the unification of Indonesia and the defense of its borders, which echoes pencak silat's role in the nation's fight for independence following World War II. Indonesia first declared its freedom on August 17, 1945, which is commemorated by *jurus tujuhbelas*, the seventeen fighting forms that are also standard repertoire for Bima Sakti's white belts.

The sempok stance's effectiveness lies in the practitioner's ability to step quickly into and leap out of position launching an attack that moves upward into the throat and abdomen of an opponent.

Having united his five brothers, Bima then led his family, the Pandawa, in defending the world from the evil Kurawa clan. Unknown to the Pandawa, their spiritual mentor, Druna, was also the Kurawa's teacher. Afraid that Bima was growing stronger and more powerful than himself, Druna sent the loyal Bima out on many dangerous missions after a fictional spring of holy water in the hopes that his student would perish at the hands of some giant or sea monster.[27] It was after one such bitter struggle that Bima awoke in the presence of the god Dewa Ruci, who asked Bima what he sought. When Bima answered that he sought a spring of holy water, the god revealed to him that there is no magic, nothing holy, except that which was inside Bima himself.[28] These powers were his sakti, the supernatural power within everyone, which is said to be the tenaga dalam employed by adherents of Bima Sakti.[29]

All of these elements may be seen in Bima Sakti's emblem. The pentagon enclosing the emblem alternately represents the five brothers of the Pandawa, the five islands of Indonesia, and the five principles of Pancasila. These elements are symbolized by the five-pointed star within the pentagon, which is used by the nation of Indonesia to represent the concept of Ketuhanan Yang Maha Esa.[30] This concept is important as, unlike prana or qi, tenaga dalam is not seen as a biological function aspiring to the physical, but quite the opposite. Reminiscent of istadewata, every practice begins with a prayer according to the personal belief of each individual. In discussions with the school's leader, Guru Besar Pak Siswanto, it was very clear he didn't believe it possible to teach an atheist. The opening of all senum, breathing exercises and sporting competitions is symbolic of taking power from God and placing it within one's heart. Only at this point can one begin to cultivate his tenaga dalam by using the mind to control the subconscious. This is a powerful and potentially dangerous practice, as illustrated by the blue and yellow of Bima Sakti's emblem. Blue is the color of the ocean and indicates depth of thinking, while the yellow is a signal for caution. Bima's hands grace the pentagon's base, reminding us of his character and strength, while the temple of Borobudur towers above, symbolizing the culture of Central Java to which Bima Sakti belongs.[31] The student of Bima Sakti must learn, in addition to his physical studies, all these elements of history, legend and symbolism. Only with this proper background may he embark upon the study of tenaga dalam.

Tenaga Dalam: The Subtle Energy

Tenaga dalam, like qi or prana, is an energy believed to exist in every individual but which needs to be awakened before it can be utilized. The first step in this awakening is various breathing techniques. Deep breaths are taken through the nose, then stored around the area of the navel, in what corresponds in Chinese medical theory to the lower *dantian*. Other techniques, like *merpati putih*, move the stored breath up and down between this point and the solar plexus (middle *dantian*) but eventually bring the air back to the navel. This technique is accomplished by tensing the abdominal muscles, often to such an extent that the body will shake and sweat profusely. An instructor will walk through a class, punching students in the stomach to ensure proper technique, as improper storage of breath will result in a weak defense during combat and can cause damage to the body's internal organs. The proper stance during these exercises is called the horse stance, though it is markedly different from that of wushu. Both emphasize a low stance, but while in wushu the purpose of the stance is to ensure stability, the opposite effect is desired in pencak silat. This is practiced, as Bima Sakti's silat style almost never uses the horse stance in a combat situation, preferring instead hollow-leg stances in which the upper torso is at a diagonal with one's opponent. While the horse stance of other martial arts has the toes point forward, this is not the case with Bima Sakti.

The moving stance used in practicing *bernafasan*. Steps are taken in a zigzag pattern. Notice that neither sole touches the floor. The uniform shown is the traditional outfit of Bima Sakti, with the insignia of Bima Sakti shown on the left, that of Ikatan Pencak Silat Indonesia (IPSI) on the right. James Wilson is here and in the technical section later in this chapter illustrating some typical movements of this martial art style.

During moving stances the toes should be at a ninety-degree angle to the direction in which one is moving. The legs should be as wide as possible, the upper leg parallel to the ground, the lower legs slightly bowed so that the sole of neither foot touches the earth. One foot should rest entirely on the inner side, while the other supports the body's weight at the outside of the foot. These foot and leg positions, which are slightly similar to those in the depok and sempok stances as well as postures of warrior characters in classical Javanese and Balinese dance, are highly unnatural, uncomfortable, and unstable. They are practiced to strengthen leg muscles and joints as well as purposely to destabilize the body. By being thrown off balance it is believed one may achieve greater awareness of the body's center of gravity. During moving stances one inhales deeply while taking his first step forward, tensing the arms as they're brought over the head from the front, arched behind the back and finally positioned in a fist at the waist. This position is then held for a slow count of ten to twenty, after which a second step is taken. Steps move in a zigzag pattern, arms proceeding in the same manner each time. A breath is taken only during the first step, however, which is then held at the navel for all subsequent steps. Exhalation in quick bursts from the nose for the purpose of discarding bad air is permissible, but no inhalations are allowed until the exercise is completed. One continues moving forward until he can no longer hold his breath, hoping to increase the number of steps with practice. The intense muscle contraction, unstable stance and holding of breath tend to bring about complete exhaustion. It is during this state that one is said to be most capable of feeling his tenaga dalam for the first time as a sensation of heat or electricity in the region of the navel.

The second step in the development of basic tenaga dalam is called *getaran*. During this exercise, one sits cross-legged, hands resting on the knees with the palms facing upward. Breathing in deeply through the nose, one once again stores air at the navel until the breath can no longer be held, by which time tenaga dalam should be felt stirring in the region of the navel. At this point slow, even breathing is resumed, inhaling through the nostrils, exhaling through the mouth. While this is being done, concentration should move from the navel up and along the right arm to the palm of the hand, which corresponds with the *laogong* cavity in Chinese acupuncture. As the mind focuses, one's tenaga dalam follows it. At first the palm of the hand feels warm or tingles; then the arm begins to move by itself, creating a sensation of floating. It is at this point that tenaga dalam begins to come under the student's control. Now, as the third step in the development of tenaga dalam is employed, a number of exercises utilizing the previously discussed breathing techniques are combined with a variety of positions taken from martial stances and yoga postures. Called *bemafasan*, these exercises serve to strengthen one's tenaga dalam while opening channels within the body so that it might be used.

Tenaga dalam has a variety of applications, which I separate into two groups: the internal, those within the body, and the external, where tenaga dalam's power and effects go beyond the body's physical limitations. I also propose that as one progresses from internal to external applications, one also progresses from the realm of reality into that of myth. The most fundamental of tenaga dalam's internal functions is that of promoting health in a manner similar to qigong. Like pencak silat's physical techniques, however, these practices seem to betray a system gathered in bits and pieces from a variety of sources, then practiced by a largely uneducated peasantry. Practices appear piecemeal as they've been handed down, with little or no explanation as to why they work. For example, placing the tongue to the palate is known in qigong to connect the conceptional and governing vessels of the body, completing the circuit known as the microcosmic orbit. This helps promote proper qi flow within the body, thereby stimulating the hormone production necessary for good health. While tongue placement is utilized in some of tenaga dalam's breathing techniques, the practice does not seem widely known. Even among those who use it, I never met anyone who understood exactly what it did or how it worked. Similarly, the practice of meditating at midnight, taken on by Daoist sages because it is the time at which the body's polarity changes, is explained on Java as the hour at which God listens to man's prayers. The degree to which God plays a role in the practice of tenaga dalam may serve the dual function of explaining aspects of qi not properly understood or investigated in Java while simultaneously providing the power perceived as being necessary for its more mythological attributes.

Still within the realm of the clearly demonstrable, however, is the use of tenaga dalam to create extreme local muscle contraction, enabling the breaking of boards, cement blocks and even iron, all of which I've witnessed. The mind over matter inherent in such feats is also manifested by practitioners holding their hands in a flame without incident. Giving testimony to the spiritual powers involved in their creation, fingerprints and the half-moon imprint of lips may still be seen in the forged metal of the Sultan's *kris*, the curved metal daggers that are Java's most characteristic weapon.

In discussing tenega dalam external manifestations, it is once again its applications with regard to healing that most resemble other common utilizations of qi. Tenaga dalam is often used to stimulate known acupressure points for therapeutic purposes in a fashion similar to qigong massage and shiatsu. While one massages these areas, tenaga dalam is literally pushed into or pulled from the patient through the fingertips or palms of the masseuse in harmony with his or her breathing and mental control. When "pushed" into a glass of water, tenaga dalam is believed to actually change the properties of the water, giving its consumption a medicinal effect. Tenaga dalam may also be used to stop even profuse bleeding without a tourniquet, applied pressure or elevation, but by simply concentrating one's power on the wound.[32] To accomplish such healing, one inhales and stores energy as described before, bringing this energy to the palm of the hand as in getaran. The moment the hand starts to "float," one slowly pushes all the air from his lungs through the mouth. The practitioner meanwhile pushes the energy out through the palm of the hand. This is done by alternately contracting and releasing the muscles along the length of the arm while simultaneously guiding the tenaga dalam to its destination with his mind. In the event of a disease caused by possessing too much energy in specific areas, which may cause certain stomach ailments, headaches and fevers, a reverse approach of inhaling and pulling the excess energy from the patient is employed. Using this same basic technique, one can place tenaga dalam anywhere, with a multitude of effects.

The most basic martial application of tenaga dalam is in harnessing the automatic movements of getaran for the improvement of reflexes while sparring. As one allows his tenaga dalam to flow freely, he tends to block automatically, anticipating his opponent's strike, thereby enabling one to fight multiple adversaries or even to fight while blindfolded. This may still be perceived within the realm of tenaga dalam's internal applications, however. Where the reaches of the imagination first begin to be stretched is in the stories of older masters, who were purported to never use physical contact when fighting, but merely to dance, using subtle blasts of tenaga dalam to confuse, bewilder and even kill their opponent. Some members of Bima Sakti claim such abilities, even after as short a time as three years of training. Dr. David Eisenberg, a clinical research fellow at Harvard Medical School and the first Westerner to study acupuncture in mainland China following Nixon's "opening" of that nation in the early 1970's, stated that, in his experience, qigong masters could barely move pieces of paper suspended on a string by use of their qi.[33] How could Javanese students of a few years be using their tenaga dalam to throw to the ground a man standing over a hundred meters away? I asked that this ability be tested on me. The teacher, Pak Siswanto, would not allow this, however, stating that someone who had not yet mastered tenaga dalam to the same degree as his opponent would face almost certain injury. The only test I was allowed to conduct was to blindfold two students, who then confronted each other at a distance of ten meters, striking only with their tenaga dalam. The students failed miserably. Not only did strikes not match reactions, but even when pointed in opposite directions they still writhed in anguish at the other's supposed attacks. Despite this disappointing evidence, however, most students continue to believe they were hitting and being hit by each other's tenaga dalam.

Even more perplexing to me is the assignment to tenaga dalam of an ability to aid in making moral distinctions. This claim is evident in the assumption that a practitioner can create an invisible force field, the first instruction for students of Bima Sakti in the use of tenaga dalam. Accomplished by means of remaining pure and asking good fortune from God[34] along with the practice of bernafasan, this general field of tenaga dalam emanates from and serves to protect the individual. Though attacked from behind, one who consistently practices these beliefs will be safe.[35] The assailant's own will, being of malicious intent, will react against him. This will be manifest in his being repelled, and even sent into convulsions until either the intended victim has moved to a safe distance or the assailant forgets his evil desire. While strong enough to repel any attack, be it from a pickpocket or a fired bullet, this general field is said not to interfere with normal interactions. Even more so, its protective power may be extended to other individuals such as friends and family or even personal belongings. Obviously, this is difficult to prove or disprove. One must simply wait until a threat occurs to him or to someone or something he has safe-guarded. Of course, one cannot choose to walk into a situation where this is liable to happen. As the Bible says, "Do not test the Lord thy God." The necessity for one to be certain of his abilities is always stressed in the study of tenaga dalam, as uncertainty leads to failure. I've known a few individuals who have broken their hands while trying to smash cinder blocks and iron rods who will attest to that.

These court servants bear incense during the ceremony of Satu Suro, the Javanese New Year, at the Hadiningrat Palace in the city of Surakarta. The city's entire population will crown the streets until the early hours of the morning to see the kingdom's royal heirlooms and magical weaponry, or *pusaka*, marched around the palace's perimeter. The selection of which pusaka will make the midnight journey is made a week in advance by members of the court after considerable meditation. The selection is determined by the weapon's appropriate magical properties necessary to cure the ills of the land during the coming year. Members of Bima Sakti participate in the ritual law as well as aid local police in security for the event. Since Suro, the first month of the Javanese calendar, is considered a time for spiritual reflection, it is taboo for mystics and martial artists who practice tenaga dalam to sleep this first night of the year. To do so is to risk malevolent spirits stealing one's powers while he slumbers.

There is one training method, however, that does attempt to prove the validity of this particular attribute of tenaga dalam. It is imperative in this practice that students work themselves into a state of emotion in which they actually feel the desire to steal an object upon which tenaga dalam has been placed. They then walk toward the object in the manner of moving stances described earlier. The tenaga dalam, reacting negatively with the student's imagined evil intent, is then felt in the area of the navel as intense heat, pain, or electrical shock. As any such experience is subjective, however, it is difficult to obtain empirical proof. I myself was never able to feel tenaga dalam in this practice, which Pak Siswanto dismissed as my inability to conjure up the emotions associated with intended theft. I witnessed many individuals cry out, fall backward, and even be seemingly thrown by these invisible forces, however, though most demonstrations seemed barely believable, almost laughable examples of poor acting. I must confess to one unique incident that proved quite the contrary, however. One day, while I was practicing silat's more conventional aspects of kicking and blocking with some friends in the south of Surakarta, a small number of people began to watch, equally intrigued with the presence of a foreigner as with our silat. In an impromptu test of tenaga dalam, we placed an invisible barrier of protection around a small boy and had him kneel down in the middle of the field where we were working out. We then took a student of Bima Sakti, who worked himself into the emotional state described above. After blindfolding him, we brought him to the area where the child sat, about twenty meters away. He then ran full force at the child, intent on pummeling him. Within inches of the boy, he seemed to hit an invisible barrier, flying over the child's head and tumbling away out of control. The child was never touched. The student then made his way carefully back to the boy, sensing the invisible force field, until he was kneeling before the child. We then watched the full grown man proceed to throw punches. Though some missed by literally fractions of an inch, not one landed. The people's faith in these powers was supported by the fact that the child and his attending father were merely passing observers unknown to any of us. I myself chose and fit the blindfold. It covered the entire face from chin to forehead. Though impressive, I must admit the experiment was far from scientific. Many questions remained. Was the student really repelled by an invisible barrier, or had he merely felt the aura of another person's qi and then leapt into his role? Had the small boy projected his thoughts, or could the student have used some form of telepathy to read the child's mind and thereby see what the boy himself was seeing? Though some force definitely seemed to be at work, there was no ascertaining what these powers might have been. Unfortunately, despite my repeated requests and the claims of other individuals, I was never able to obtain a remotely satisfactory reproduction of this demonstration.

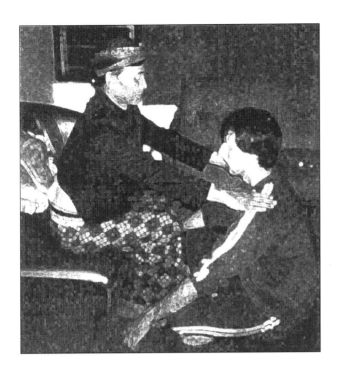

The author undergoing initiation into Bima Sakti under the hand of Guru Besar Pak F.L. Siswanto, the school's founder.

This photograph above shows a reenactment. The actual event was not allowed to be photographed, not for reasons of secrecy, but because the forces present, according to Pak Siswanto, could possibly burn the film or cause the flash or lenses to explode. The entire initiation encompasses three days of progressive ritual, during which the initiate is not allowed to practice either alone or with other silat members. At midnight entering the first day, the initiate must bathe completely. Beginning this day, one must also start to "lessen" his pleasures. He must abstain from favorite foods, sexual relations, frivolous activities, and the like. From sunset of the second day on, the initiate fasts from everything except water.

At sunset of the third day the initiate arrives at Pak Siswanto's house, where an older Bima Sakti instructs him or her in the order of the evening's events. The initiate spends the first hour alone in meditation upon all the wrongdoing of his life as far back as he can remember, mentally asking forgiveness from God (according to the individual's own beliefs) and those parties wronged by each particular sin. After the meditation the initiate proceeds into a room where Pak Siswanto sits in full traditional Javanese dress, including his sacred kris. Upon entering the room the initiate states his complete name three times, then sits cross-legged on the floor before Pak Siswanto, who proceeds to present the initiate verbally to God (Ketuhanan Yang Maha Era). Following this ritual, both parties stand, after which Pak Siswanto presents various body parts to God for the purpose of doing good, each time exhaling his tenaga dalam while the initiate breathes this energy in, to awaken his own "inner force."

The author with Susuhunan (King) Pukubuwana XII
during the ceremony of Satu Suro in 1991.

The first body part presented is the mind. While breathing out, Pak Siswanto presses down on the top of the initiate's head over what correlates in Chinese acupuncture with the *baihui* cavity (which is also "breathed through" in some qigong meditations). Second, the body or torso is presented, Pak Siswanto's middle finger being pressed into the initiate's shoulders at a point corresponding to the *tianliao*. Third, the hands are presented and pressed into the palms at the *laogong* cavity, then an application is given to the legs and feet. The hands are merely passed over these extremities. The author experienced sensations during this procedure similar to those described by acupuncture patients during treatment. Following this ritual the initiate and Pak Siswanto leave the room. The student washes his hands in water poured from a brass urn into a bowl filled with scented water and red and white rose petals. The act symbolizes the washing of sin from his life. Then the initiate breaks the fast with a ceremonial meal, after which he takes oaths, the basic purpose of which is the upholding of the principles of Pencasila. The ritual meal consists of the following foods listed with their associated meaning.

The placement of tenaga dalam upon inanimate objects needn't only be for the object's protection, however. It can also, in the case of particularly powerful mystics, imbue such objects with magical powers. This was mentioned previously with regard to the Javanese kris, the craftsmen of which would leave their fingerprints in the blade's molten metal, or cool it with their lips. Few men are still alive who possess the magic necessary for the creation of truly powerful blades.[36]

Ceremonial Meal

Water = Purity

Milk = Health

Chicken Heart = Fidelity

"King" Banana = Confidence

"Semar" Biscuit = Semar, a messenger between heaven and earth.

Red & White
Sticky Rice = The colors of the rose petals in which the student wahes his hands, symbollizing the Javanese principles of male and female, the yin and yang. In contemporary Indonesia these are the colors of the nation's flag, and represent the loyalty of the people and the blood they were willing to shed for its freedom.

Such blades constituted the *pusaka*, or magical weaponry, of a kingdom. This weaponry was held in such high esteem that often, when one Javanese kingdom conquered another, rather than razing its *kraton* or stealing its wealth, the victor would simply acquire the other's pusaka. From that point on, the defeated monarch would cease to be a threat, having been rendered impotent as a ruler. His magic gone, no one would follow him. While the pusaka's extraordinary powers can make a kingdom strong, it also takes a spiritually strong ruler to possess such pusaka.[37] The plethora of pusaka amassed by Sultan Agung helped greatly in strengthening his rule. Conversely, a king who lost his pusaka, even if he remained on the throne, was seen by the masses as lacking the spiritual fortitude necessary to govern.

The widespread belief in pusaka undoubtedly came about during the beginning of the Islamic era for the political and sociological reasons presented previously in discussing the circumstances surrounding the Mataram Empire's legitimization. This Islamic influence may be borne out by the fact that the most common form of *jimat* were Islamic prayers written on a scrap of cloth, wrapped around a piece of brass or copper, and sewn into the lining of one's clothing.[38] Jimat and pusaka were highly regarded in the absence of comparable fire power during Indonesia's revolution against the Dutch (1945–49). One guerilla leader is reputed to have inserted magical needles into his skin, which then circulated throughout his body, making him invulnerable to attack. When Dutch troops stormed the Mangkunegaran Palace in Surakarta, the prince is believed to have merely waved his kris, leaving them petrified, unable to move for hours. When he set them free, they ran away in terror. Even deceased revolutionaries such as Diponegoro were said to have aided in the battle, the inner strength of their departed spirits supposedly bringing down Dutch war planes that flew over their graves.[39] Because of the spiritual power that could be gathered at such places, pencak silat brotherhoods began to form and train in the graveyards of Java under secret oaths of loyalty to the gods, the spirits of the past, the brotherhood, and the people of a budding nation. Powerful jimat and powers of tenaga dulam were allegedly conferred upon members with the taking of these vows. Still common in Java are the legends of unarmed martial artists who, when fired upon, merely caught the bullets and swallowed them like berries. The Sultan of Yogyakarta himself is purported to have feasted on a bomb he turned into jackfruit after the Dutch dropped it, ineffectually, on his palace.

Psychiatrist turned dissenting journalist, Frantz Fanon explained the origin of similar stories in his own native homeland of Martinique and later in Algeria during these nations' struggles against the French. According to Fanon, a colonized society is constantly being told it is inferior, not only militarily, but culturally. The only way for an oppressed individual to become socially mobile is to adopt the values of the oppressor, a tacit acknowledgment of the oppressor's superiority. This was definitely true in the system of aristocratic bureaucracy the Dutch installed in Indonesia. The only man considered educated was the one who wore European style clothes and spoke Dutch. A great fantasy for a person of color was to be white; there was nothing inherently desirable in being Indonesian.

Fanon summarized his dilemma as a second-class citizen in his own country in the following manner: "When people like me, they tell me it is in spite of my color. When they dislike me, they point out that it is not because of my color. Either way I am locked into the infernal circle."[40]

Until the oppressed resurrect their pride as a people through the successful removal of the powers of subjugation, they must seek to transcend this "infernal circle" and gain a sense of self-worth in some other manner. Fanon noted a return to ancient religions and the creation of myths regarding great feats of strength and magic. To this day, almost any villager in Java will say the Dutch were ousted by virtue of Indonesia's superior strength, especially its magical power, citing the examples I gave above. No explanation is offered as to why Indonesia, possessing such powers, endured over three centuries of Dutch rule, however. The truth is that the Japanese removed the Dutch during their occupation of the islands in World War II. When the Dutch tried to return after the war, they were overwhelmed by sheer numbers. The resources necessary to retake the archipelago proved economically unfeasible for the post-war Netherlands, and the bloodshed incurred would have been condemned by the international community. The U.N. Security Council, amid Dutch protests, had already unanimously called for a cease-fire on August 1, 1947, two years before the fighting would actually stop.

Indonesian independence was, therefore, not the result of a glorious uprising won by magical force, but a product of the circumstances of World War II, world sentiment against imperialism, and the valiant shedding of blood and laying down of lives by thousands of brave Indonesians. For many, however, the first version is more glorious and less painful and erases the embarrassment of 350 years of colonial rule. And so, the Javanese penchant for myth-making, which legitimized the ascendance of Mataram's peasant kings, also acted as the magic feather enabling Indonesia's triumph over a superior Dutch military. The powers drawn from Java's religious and mystic heritage, be they real or imagined, continue to instill a sense of pride in the people of Indonesia. They serve to confirm their country's greatness, even when beleaguered by overwhelming hardship.[41] As Gusti Parto, son of Susuhunan Paku Buwana XII, one of the rulers of the former Mataram Empire, stated:

> Every nation is known for one thing, one export. France is fashion. America, democracy. Japan is technology, like cars and cameras. Indonesia is a poor nation, but we are rich. We have not yet found our export, but here we can heal a man without any medicine. We can turn invisible, defeat an opponent without touching him, and travel great distances with merely the power of our minds.

In this way, schools of pencak silat will continue to unite their country and protect her borders. They will do so by providing the sense of uniqueness and spiritual fortitude necessary for Indonesia to maintain its cultural integrity during the gargantuan task of attaining economic prosperity and technological modernization. To the degree that this task is accomplished, tenaga dalam, ilmu, kekuatan and all forms of magic on the island of Java are validated in every aspect. Like any martial art, victory is not only a matter of power, but faith.

Artwork © Pop Vichaya
Facebook.com/Pop315Photography

Technical Section
THE FIVE BASIC STRIKES OF LIMA POKOK
which also symbolize the principles of Pancasila.

Ia All strikes are executed from this basic stance in which the front leg is hollow, prepared to be pulled back and lash out at the groin or midsection. The striking hand is kept in a fist at the waist, and the forward hand, thumb tucked in, serves to protect and guard the eyes so as not to divulge one's intentions to their enemy. The torso faces forward at an angle.

Ib As one steps forward, the first strike, actually a block, is thrown, the back arm coming forward, sweeping the forearm up to force to the outside an incoming strike to the head or torso. The forearm sweeps downward to protect the abdomen and groin.

Ic A roundhouse punch, center knuckle forward, is directed at the temple.

Id/e The third strike is an open-hand attack is aimed at the solar plexus, the soft flesh of the throat just beneath the Adam's apple, or directly between the eyes. Shown here in two photographs, the strike is executed palm up, the hand rotating at the last moment with the intention of creating a ripping motion with the fingers and nails, tearing open the flesh of an opponent. The fourth strike, a close-fisted, straight punch, is executed with the exact same motion.

If The last attack is a chop originating from behind the ear, directed at the opponent's collar bone.

Pembukaan

The opening for all practices, competitions, bernafasan and senam exercises.

2a From a standing position with arms at sides,

2b inhale, raising arms over head and bringing hands together, right thumb crossing over left (the body's energy passes from right hand to left), then

2c holding breath, bring hands straight down to stop level with the sternum, symbolizing bringing the power of God (Ketuhanan Yang Maha Esa) into the practitioner's own heart.

Bernafasan Series One

3a From this position, the lower the better, torso erect, inhale, storing breath and energy in the abdomen (dantian), simultaneously clenching hands into fists, contracting the muscles of the arms, shoulders and abdomen. Neck and face should remain relaxed, however.

3b The fists should be held at the waist while the breath is held. When exhaling, do so slowly, pushing the arms forward, palms open and facing out, mentally pushing one's tenaga dalam up from the stomach, down the arms, and out the palms with one's breath, and then return to position in 3A. Relax the arms and repeat two more times. Not only does this strengthen the arms, legs and torso, but is also practice for thrusting one's tenaga dalam at an opponent, enabling the martial artist to strike from a distance. Theoretically such a force can be employed to cause internal damage and illness to an enemy at any distance, be it kilometers or continents away.

3c Completing the exercise shown in Figures 3A and 3B, proceed to the same hollow leg stance utilized in demonstrating lima pokok, right foot forward, right hand relaxed, palm open, in line with the right leg. The left hand is raised, palm up as if holding a platter, palm level with shoulder about six inches behind the body.

3d Inhale, drawing the right hand back until the middle finger is about two inches above and pointing at the left palm. Store the breath and energy, contracting the muscles of the right arm, shoulder and abdomen as before. The left hand remains relaxed. Picture a ball of energy being held in the upturned palm of the left hand. Exhale slowly, returning the right arm to the position shown in Figure 3C, simultaneously pushing energy from the stomach down the arm and out the tip of the middle finger. Picture the energy from the left palm being carried in an arc along the fingertips of the right hand. This is also repeated three times. Then switch to the left leg forward and repeat three times again. This exercise is to practice the muscle and energy control required for breaking tiles, cinder blocks and iron bars with one's bare hands, with obvious uses in combat.

3e Return to the original stance as shown in Figure 3A. Inhale, pulling the arms up and behind, contracting muscles and storing breath as before.

3f Exhale, bringing the arms down, right crossing over left.

3g Inhale, raising the arms over the head, then down to the waist in a fist, as in Figure 3B.

3h Exhale, pushing the arms forward to return to the position shown in Figure 3A. Repeat the entire process three times. This exercise serves to build strength and stamina in the legs, reinforces the exercise in Figures 3A and 3B, and helps strengthen the torso to withstand attack. (No photo).

3i Returning to a standing position, inhale, bringing the right fist up to meet the left palm in front of the heart. The fist symbolizes the power of the martial artist, the palm stopping the fist being a promise not to use this power irresponsibly.

3j Exhaling, the exercise is brought to a close by bringing the fist and palm down to the right side, like holstering a weapon. This signifies not only the end of bernafasan, but also senam or any pencak silat competition.

Notes

1 Buck, W. (trans.). (1973). *Mahabharata*. Berkeley: University of California Press, p. 79.

2 Just as the statement ". . . all men are created equal. . ." is integral to American identity, belief in One True God (Ketuhanan Yang Maha Esa) is the cornerstone of Indonesian nationalism. It is the first of the nation's five guiding principles, called *Pancasila* (*panca* meaning five; *sila* meaning principle).

3 Women have been prominent throughout pencak silat's development. The style currently most popular in Indonesia is that of Merpati Putih, which means 'white dove,' but is also a Javanese acronym meaning "good conduct obtained through silence." Merpati Putih's fighting forms are said to have been the creation of an

anonymous daughter of the eighteenth century Javanese Prince Mangkubumi of Yogyakarta.

4 The use of tenaga dalam to create barriers, or force fields, is one of the unique traits that separate it from a traditional understanding of qi, and will be explored later.

5 Repeated prayers with magical properties, typically not in Indonesian, but regional dialects or archaic language forms no longer used in everyday speech.

6 The *dukun* is the Indonesian shaman. Well-versed in the ways of the natural and supernatural, his purported powers range from fortune telling and herbal healing to powerful hexes and raising people from the dead. His role in dances such as Dayakan is to protect everyone involved from both physical and spiritual harm.

7 These chakra points roughly correspond to the reproductive organs, intestines, solar plexus, thymus, thyroid and pituitary glands, and the cerebral cortex.

8 Islam literally means "to submit."

9 The fact that the Dutch did control Indonesia so completely, with frequent animosity between native and colonial forces, may explain why, despite their presence in the archipelago for 350 years, Christians still account for less than five percent of the population.

10 The first example of this, the Hindu Sanjaya, became so convinced that Shiva and Buddha were the same that, even after they regained autonomy from the Buddhist Sailendra dynasty, they continued to incorporate Buddhist motifs on their Hindu temples and even completed the construction of Borobudur.

11 This creation, though modern scholars find its lineages and histories riddled with inconsistencies, proved worthy of acceptance by the Dutch establishment in Java just twenty years after Senapati's recorded death. He is still considered by most Javanese to be the first ruler of Mataram.

12 Muslim religious leaders and saints. In Islam there is no separation between church and state, a fact which necessitates their abolition if Rangsang was to have free reign over his empire.

13 *Ngoko, Madya, Krama.* These may be combined to create further divisions for various social occasions, and a fourth, *krama ingil,* is a modified form of krama only used in reference to royalty and divinity.

14 Spiritual force, esoteric knowledge and inner strength, respectively.

15 For an example, examine Ibn' Arabi's interpretation of the story of Noah (see bibliography).

16 This toleration of other expressions of the divine Dharma solidified the concept of *ketuhanan,* and also established the Javanese idea of *istadewata,* the personal god of choice.

17 Ibn' Arabi stated that anyone who experienced *kashf* would typically be mute

for several days following the event.

[18] Izutsu, T. (1983). *Sufism and Taoism: A comparative study of key philosophical concepts*. Berkeley: University of California Press.

[19] Pak Anom Suroto of Surakarta, considered by most to be Indonesia's foremost *dalang*, is a member of the school of Bima Sakti and a practitioner of tenaga dalam.

[20] Before a performance is begun, reminiscent of Java's shamanistic tradition, offerings of spiced meats, rice and a live rooster are placed as a sacrifice to ward off evil spirits. Incense is burned to invoke the blessings of ancestors, spirits and *Ketuhanan*. Ketuhanan, the undifferentiated Absolute, is symbolized by the burning oil lamp that shines its light upon the leather puppets, the divine archetypes as manipulated by God, symbolized by the dalang.

The screen is the universe, the world as we know it. The pole on the left, from which all the evil characters are drawn, represents the negative, and the pole to the right, where the heroes stand, represents the positive. Both poles serve the function of holding up the screen, of supporting the universe, however, and are equally necessary. When the light of the Absolute falls upon the archetypes manipulated by God, their shadows fall upon the universe. For the audience on the other side, these shadows are but mysteries, simple black and white, good and evil, giving no clues as to the events that might unfold. But should a spectator come and watch from behind the screen, he would see that the mere shadows are actually brightly painted puppets, and their colors warn if they're happy or angry, coming in peace or going to war. From here one can watch the dalang, can see God, and know his play, understand dharma. This is the role of trance in Javanese society, to cross to the other side of the shadow screen. But one can never understand the Absolute, for if one looks into the bright flame of the oil lamp, what can be seen? Nothing. He is blinded. It lies beyond comprehension, for everything, including God, lies within the Absolute.

[21] This practice is undoubtedly derived from the character Rama from the much loved *Ramayana* epic. Unlike their Hindu counterparts, however, the goal of such denial among the satria was to have a spiritual encounter with Javanese shamanistic deities. The most popular of these were Ratu Kidul, Queen of the South Sea and supposed wife and benefactor of the kings of Mataram, or Semar, the clown-god who dwells in a cave atop Dieng Plateau at the heart of the island and is said to watch over all of Java. Chapters of the Merpati Putih school of pencak silat near the city of Yogyakarta still spend a full night of meditation in the caves of Parangtritis, the home of Ratu Kidul. Members of Bima Sakti, based in Surakarta, must walk barefoot in the dead of night forty kilometers from Tawang Mangu, a waterfall on the slopes of Mount Lawu, back to the city before

being able to receive their yellow belt.

[22] While fasting is believed to be a form of bodily and spiritual cleansing, in Javanese mysticism it is also perceived as a means of payment, when used with mantras, for a variety of magical powers. These vary from levitation and invisibility to the possession of animal familiars and the ability to travel inside a beam of light. Ritual fasting for spiritual maintenance is also utilized. This may be fasting from spices, meat, coffee or any designated item on assigned days of the week. It also includes fasting from certain staples like rice during a particular month or season. A common practice is a complete fast from all nourishment one day a month on the date of one's birthday according to the Javanese calendar. More rigorous fasts include the forty-day fast or the often fatal practice of *bertapa*. This latter practice, supposedly yielding great powers and enlightenment, involves total sensory deprivation. The individual undertaking Besar Pak Siswanto is buried sitting cross-legged under the earth for an indeterminate amount of time, a bamboo straw providing air from the surface. During the summer of 1992, newspapers reported the deaths of two young men who had taken on the endeavor together. A third individual survived.

[23] Breathing techniques employing localized tightening of muscles is combined with *sabun tulang*, or bone washing, for the physical conditioning necessary to accomplish this passive blocking. Sabun tulang cultivates hard-style blocks, strikes and kicks against wooden, metal or stone targets for the purpose of conditioning. This practice is also demonstrated in breaking such objects, which will be discussed later. In more traditional settings, displays similar to *debus* may be witnessed. Donn Draeger spoke of such an event in his book, *The Weapons and Fighting Arts of Indonesia* (p. 165): "Precombat, all aspiring participants inflict wounds upon their own chest and abdomen, usually using the kris in stabbing and slashing fashion. The combatants thus develop a high threshold against pain which is to come in the actual fight. Music, percussion type, with a spirited rhythm sets the stage for all preliminary rituals. Some form of autosuggestion or self-hypnosis is probably the method by which the trances and frenzied condition of the combatants are achieved. The self-inflicted kris lacerations made during the precombat period are highly valued. Examination of the combatants during the precombat trances showed that only their forearms were tense or rigid; above the elbows they were relaxed. The precombat state was one of calm, but as the fight neared, the calmness was shattered and a near hysteria developed. Shouting and screaming accompanied the combats. Incense was burned during the entire weird affair."

[24] Java, Sumatra, Kalimantan, Sulawesi and Irian Jaya.

[25] The symbol of four becoming complete in the fifth, adopted by the Javanese, is

a common concept in Hindu numerology. The four *dhatu*, or humors (wind, bile, phlegm and blood), unite to make a fifth entity, the human body, which creates and is created by the previous four, thereby uniting five into one, The gods of the four compass points are united in the fifth point, the center, which is the Oneness of Shiva. Four thereby becomes a number to be avoided, as it lacks completeness. In gamelan there are two scales; one, the *slendro*, is characterized by five tones, while in the seven-note pelog scale the fourth tone is rarely played, except toward the end of a piece to create a feeling of irresolution before the tonic is struck.

[26] 1) Belief in One True God (Ketuhanan Yang Maha Esa); 2) A benevolent humanity, this being the responsibility of each individual; 3) National unity (Bhinneka Tunggal Ika); 4) The sovereignty of the people through representation and consensus, and; 5) Social justice, meaning the prosperity of the people.

[27] Stories such as this may partially betray a general mistrust of religious and mystic teachers that can still be sensed in Java to this day. Because of the circumstances surrounding the island's sociological and religious evolution, the Javanese tend to stick tenaciously to their tradition of syncretism in the face of any imposed dogmas. Indeed, though there are general traits, specific doctrine or practices concerning Javanese mysticism cannot be said to exist, as everyone will give a different version. This is because in Javanese mysticism, known as *kebatinan*, one's teacher is only there to help him hear the voice of the spirit, or batin, within him. Once this is done, one's batin becomes his teacher, which in turn leads each individual on his own uniquely predetermined path.

[28] This marks a unique trait of Bima Sakti in contrast with other forms of pencak silat, in that it does not use anything outside of tenaga dalam, such as mantra or possession. These are believed to be inferior to tenaga dalam and possibly even harmful or evil.

[29] As an interesting side note, Bima Sakti does not only mean the supernatural power of Bima, but is also the Indonesian appellation for our galaxy, known in the West as the Milky Way.

[30] This is not the five-pointed star of Islam as some may think. Many of Bima Sakti's members in Surakarta are, in fact, Catholic.

[31] It is interesting to note that according to popular legend, Borobudur, the world's largest ancient structure in the southern hemisphere, was constructed in a single night by its architect, Gunadharma, using a power not unlike tenaga dalam. *Guna* means "to use"; thus the name Gunadharma literally means "to use dharma."

[32] It is interesting to note that certain gifted women, usually elderly, would be kept on call in the coal mines of Pennsylvania and the Appalachians well into the

59

present century because of their ability to stop bleeding in precisely this way.

[33] Eisenberg, D., with T. Wright. (1985). *Encounters with chi*. New York: W.W. Norton & Co.

[34] Once again, whatever God one may believe in.

[35] I hesitate to use the word "techniques," as it is the moral purity and prayer which are key here.

[36] Such men were not only spiritual masters and skilled craftsmen, but also knowledgeable alchemists, blending metals into strong alloys. The royal kris of Surakarta may always be distinguished by their *pamur*, or luster, which is provided by the materials taken from a meteorite that fell near the temples of Prambanan. This meteorite is now contained in the maze of the kraton's inner sanctuary. Scientists have analyzed it and found it consists of a rather remarkable alloy, its incredible strength perfect for creating a trustworthy weapon.

[37] Some kris were said to be able to fly of their own accord to slay a victim, render their bearer invisible once unsheathed, or quiver in the presence of evil, among other attributes.

[38] Inanimate objects that similarly bestow magical powers upon their owners. While pusaka are found in the kratons, jimt are located among the lower strata of society.

[39] Diponegoro (1787–1855), led a brilliant but unsuccessful five year military campaign against the Dutch establishment on Java (1825–30).

[40] Fanon, F. (1968). *Black skin, white masks*. New York: Grove Press, p. 116.

[41] This condition of overwhelming hardship continues even in post-revolutionary Indonesia. In the mid-1960's when millions of Indonesians were starving and inflation was hovering around 700%, the nation's first president, Sukarno, was building monuments and sports arenas where he gave speeches about Indonesia's supremacy among nations. Legend states that, when Sukarno set his hat down at the U.N., no other world leader could lift it, so strong was his ilmu, and that when a gunman went to shoot Sukarno while he was praying, many images of him appeared, causing the gunman to miss (Sukarno did survive such an assassination attempt, as well as three others, two involving hand grenades, and a third when he was attacked by a fighter plane). In the midst of growing public sentiment against government corruption, especially that perpetrated by the family of Indonesia's second and most current president, Suharto, there has been a resurgence of both traditional magic and Islamic fundamentalism among the poor that constitute the majority of the nation's populace. In 1976, a retired high school teacher received the backing of national religious leaders in his claim that he had received a divine sign to rule. He created quite a stir in Suharto's administration and an investigation into its validity. Faced by a lack of genuine

economic or political empowerment, the people of Java have provided themselves with a very real sense of control over their destiny through imagined supernatural powers.

Bibliography

Bianchi, E. (1972). *The religious experience of revolutionaries*. New York: Doubleday and Company.

Buck, W. (trans.). (1973). *Mahabharata*. Berkeley: University of California Press.

Campbell, J. (1962). *The masks of God: Oriental mythology*. New York: Penguin Books.

Campbell, J. (1959). *The masks of God: Primitive mythology*. New York: Penguin Books.

Chia, M. (1983). *Awaken healing energy through the Tao*. Santa Fe, New Mexico: Aurora Press.

Chopra, D., Sharma, H., and Dev Triguna, B. (May 22, 1991). Maharishi Ayur-Veda: Modern insights into ancient medicine. *Journal of the American Medical Association*, 265(20), 2633–2637.

Conze, E. (trans.) (1959). *Buddhist scriptures*. London: Penguin Classics.

Couteau, J. (November, 1990). Garuda: From myth to national symbol. *The Archipelago*, 1:10–17

Draeger, D. (1972). *The weapons and fighting arts of Indonesia*. Tokyo: Charles E. Tuttle Publishing Co., Inc.

Dumarcay, J. (1978). *Borobodur*. New York: Oxford University Press.

Eisenberg, D., with Lee Wright, T. (1985). *Encounters with qi*. New York: Penguin Books, Ltd.

Fanon, F. (1968). *Black skin, white masks*. New York: Grove Press, p. 116.

Fink, J. (November, 1990). Balinese tolerance. *The Archipelago*.

Griveti, L. (February, 1991). Nutrition Past—Nutrition today: The prescientific origins of nutrition and dietetics. (Part 1: The nutritional dietary legacy of India). *Nutrition Today*.

Haditjaroko, S. (1962). *Ramuyana: Indonesian wayang show*. Indonesia: Djambatan.

Hefner, R. (1985). *Hindu Javanese*. Princeton, New Jersey: Princeton University Press.

Izutsu, T. (1983). *Sufism and Taoism: A comparative study of key philosophical concepts*. Los Angeles: University of California Press.

Kartodirdjo, S. (1988). *Modern Indonesia: Tradition and transformation*. Yogyakarta, Indonesia: Gadjah Mada University Press.

Kosut, H. (ed.) (1967). *Indonesia: The Sukarno years*. New York: Facts on File

Publications.

Lee, K. (1976). *Indonesia: Between myth and reality*. London: Nile Mackenzie.

Moedjanto, G. (1990). *The concept of power in Javanese culture*. Yogyakarta, Indonesia: Gadjah Mada University Press.

Mulder, N. (1989). *Individual and society in Java: A cultural analysis*. Yogyakarta, Indonesia: Gadjah Mada University Press.

Parrinder, G. (1971). *World religions from ancient history to the present*. New York: Facts on File Publications.

Soekmono, R. (1976). *Chandi Borobodur*. Paris: The Unesco Press.

Vittachi, T. (1967). *The fall of Sukarno*. New York: Praeger, Publishers.

Xiu, R. (September 23, 1988). Microcirculation and traditional Chinese medicine. *Journal of the American Medical Association*.

Yang, J., and Bolt, J. (1982). *Shaolin long fist kung fu*. Burbank, CA: Unique Publications Inc.

Yang, J. (1989). *The root of Chinese chi kung*. Boston: YMAA.

Zimmer, H. (1948). *Hindu medicine*. Baltimore: Johns Hopkins University Press Reprints.

Silat Kebatinan as an Expression of Mysticism and Martial Culture in Southeast Asia

by Mark V. Wiley

Illustrations by Carlos Aldrete.

Since it is embraced in wrappings spun by various religious sects, the full significance of kebatinan may be obscured even though it maintains its socio-cultural identity. Although *kebatinan* is the final stage of one's study of the indigenous martial art known as *silat* (Draeger & Smith, 1980; Maliszewski, 1992; Sheikh, 1994), its practice is not limited to the *pesilat* (ind., practitioner of silat).[1] Adding to this confusion is the fact that one's kebatinan practice may be steeped in Islam, Hinduism, Buddhism, or any other religious or mystical movement—or variation thereof—including the practice of black and white magic, although such magical practices are frowned upon by the "true" possessor of kebatinan (Stange, 1980; Sheikh, 1994). In fact, as Mulder (1982: 105) notes: "Basically, kebatinan is mysticism, the penetration and the knowledge of the universe with the purpose of establishing a direct relationship between the individual and the sphere of That-Which-Is-Almighty."

It is at this time that I make the distinction between kebatinan movements and variants. A kebatinan movement can be any "school" of thought rooted in a specific religion such as Hinduism, for example. Conversely, variants include those "schools" whose disciples actively depart from the traditional norms of their religion for personal gain, a practice that may constitute a violation of their major religious code.[2] This characterization of kebatinan may not necessarily be accepted by all those who practice it. However, since I neither practice kebatinan nor have witnessed its effects in person,[3] this is how I can best understand and therefore communicate its essence. As with the explanations of traditional peoples who may describe their mystical expression, this explanation is based on my own ethnocentric, compartmentalized worldview. Therefore, any researcher who may use this thesis as a guide is advised to cross reference my interpretations of the references included herein. Because of the vast number of kebatinan movements observed in Southeast Asia, this treatment will offer a mere overview of three of the more common *aliran* (ind., mystical movements or sects), namely the *abangan*, *santri*, and *sumarah*, while focusing on the aspects of those variants which are relevant to the study of Indo-Malayan martial culture.

" . . . kebatanan is . . .
a direct relationship between
the individual and the sphere
of That-Which-Is-Almight."
—Moulder (1982: 105)

Aliran Kebatinan: An Overview

Kebatinan (arb., integrated into ind., jav.: *batin*, inner, internal, in the heart, hidden and mysterious; *kebatinan*, the science of the "batin") is observed and practiced in Southeast Asia. It is a spiritual path which seeks to develop an inner tranquility through one's total submission and self-surrender to God—any god. Kebatinan is commonly ascribed to mysticism in general and/or those movements relating to it (Stange, 1980; Mulder, 1982).

Although there are many kebatinan movements and variants observed today, the general practice of this Southeast Asian mystical expression can be divided into two basic categories. One type involves the practice of the indigenous Southeast Asian martial art known as *silat*, which involves two dimensions: human (e.g., corporeal) and supernatural (e.g., the spirits of angels or culture heroes). In silat, the acquisition of a mystical "energy" is sought. This "energy" is obtained through the practice of specific breathing exercises known as *dzikir* (Sharif, 1990;[4] Maliszewski, 1992). The other type of mystical expression is solely concerned with the dimensions of God, all upon which an "inner" knowing and/or an "internal" awareness is developed through the strict observance of prayer and ritual. Again, these prayers and rituals may assume any number of forms depending on the faith to which one subscribes and the particular aliran of which one is a member.

The *abangan kebatinan* variant is rooted in the animistic aspects of Javanism,[5] in particular the peasant element (Geertz, 1960). Although nominally Muslim, the individuals who follow this variant often find their religious inspiration in the Javanism complex associated with animistic, Hindu, Buddhist magical-mystical-religious elements (Mulder, 1970b). The abangan variant, regardless of religious doctrine, connects the sociocultural beliefs with the all-encompassing cosmic order that is "Life." Inspired by the *wayang kulit*[6] depicted in the *Mahabharata*, the abangan variant views life in the here and now as a mere shadow of the events occurring on a higher plane (Mangkunagara VII of Surakarta, 1957; Mulder, 1982).

The *santri kebatinan* variant, which is followed by the Islam *putihan*, or strict adherents of Islam, also includes within its practice various elements of Javanism (Mulder, 1970b). This further shows how the practice of this mystical endeavor can at times be directed toward a closer relationship with God through a specific religious realm (e.g., Islam) and at other times step outside of the pertinent religious ideals to achieve the goals of the individual practitioner. According to Geertz (1960: 6), the santri variant of kebatinan represents "a stress on the Islamic aspects of the syncretism and is generally related to the trading element [merchant class] (and to certain elements in the peasantry as well)."

The variant known as *sumarah kebatinan*, not unlike other variants, is said to cultivate a state of total surrender or submission, the inwardly receptive state of being (Stange, 1980). However, whereas other variants seem to deal predominantly with a state of internal awareness and self-control, the sumarah movement attempts to direct its energies at changing social patterns in an effort to invoke a greater communal harmony. Indonesians view sumarah kebatinan as a mechanism which enables them to focus on the social interactions which exist between group consciousness and one's culture at large (Stange, 1981).

Kebatinan as Worldview

Worldview can be thought of as the way in which a people view the world, the customs and beliefs of other people, and their relation to the supernatural. Worldview is an all-encompassing, abstract framework for one's life experiences and for ones interpretations of those experiences. Indeed, worldview and religion in Southeast Asia are at once inseparable and syncretic, as noted by Mulder (1970a: 79):

> In most traditional, rather undifferentiated societies, religious practice and belief still provide most of the vital coordinates of a worldview. The sociological and psychological importance of a worldview is that it shapes the attitude of life of individuals; a worldview can therefore be studied as revealing the approach to reality of individuals and groups, which means that it can be analyzed as the logic behind a social system and its dynamics.

However, one distinction needs to be made concerning the observance of religion proper and kebatinan. Whereas the practice of kebatinan attempts to connect the concept of an "inner" man with God, religion adheres to the necessity of an intermediary between man and God (e.g., a prophet, priest, or the written word as presented in the Holy Bible) (Mulder, 1970b).

Anyone may participate in the practice of kebatinan. It is pursued generally to get away from the oppressive social ties, to attain inner tranquility, and to escape the dogma of organized religions (Mulder, 1970b).

Southeast Asian Martial Culture: An Overview

Perhaps one of the best examples of how kebatinan is expressed is through an analysis of Southeast Asian martial arts forms. Most of our understanding in the West concerning these fighting forms relies strictly upon physical movement. Yet in Asia, physical, philosophical, religious, and spiritual expressions also permeate the practice of martial arts. This is probably best seen in Indonesian and Malayan systems of silat. However, a brief introduction to a discussion of silat in Southeast Asian martial arts is in order.

In general, many Asian martial traditions are believed to have originated in India. This belief is supported by the many martial episodes within the pages of such Indian epics as the *Mahabharata* and *Ramayana*. Since Indonesia has been subjected to the cultural and martial influences of India, China, and Indochina (Draeger, 1972; Draeger and Smith, 1980; Maliszewski, 1992), it is no wonder that its martial culture is laced with a plethora of mystical beliefs and practices. Maliszewski (1987, 1992) further notes that Java, Indonesia's cultural and political core, has always been a center of magical and mystical beliefs. With the gaining of independence from the Dutch in 1949 and the ongoing migrations of the Indo-Malayan peoples, there has developed a very sophisticated Southeast Asian combative form collectively known as silat—although there are literally hundreds of silat variants or styles practiced on the Indonesian Archipelago and the Malay Peninsula. Because West Java is the current hub of Indonesian silat, it is no surprise that this martial tradition maintains the practice of kebatinan as its highest level.

Although other combatives are found in this geographic region, e.g., *pukulan*, *kuntao*, and various "endemic" forms, Draeger (1972), Stange (1980), and Maliszewski (1987, 1992) note that silat is, in fact, the major self-defense system practiced and the one with the strongest spiritual, religious, and mystical roots. "As a formal tradition, spiritual components of silat are known to have developed through contact with Hindu and Islamic teachings" (Maliszewski, 1992: 27). Draeger (1972) expounds on this idea by asserting that in ancient times the *pendeta* (ind., priests) used to study animal movements from which contemporary silat derives much of its physical form. He further notes that it was the combination of the physical animal actions coupled with various meditative postures which provided the priests with the necessary skills of self-defense. These meditative postures and other spiritual practices were said to have derived from the Tantric and Sufi traditions (Stange, 1980).

The initiation into and the practice of silat is an interesting progression of patience, ritual, and physicality. Draeger and Smith (1980) note that a prospective student must first negotiate with a silat *guru* (ind., teacher) in order to be accepted as his pupil. The pupil must then adhere to tradition by carrying five offerings to the guru at his training pavilion. These offerings include, but are not limited to, a chicken whose blood is spread on the training ground as a symbolic substitute for blood that might otherwise come from the student and a roll of white cloth in which to wrap the corpse if a student should die in training. After a student has been accepted into a particular silat system, he would then undergo a strenuous training progression, which would include the practice of various stances, postures, strikes, blocks, memorized patterns of movements, and sparring practice (Draeger, 1972; Draeger & Smith, 1980; Stange, 1980; Maliszewski, 1987, 1992). The idea is that the student of silat is naive and young (in a spiritual sense) and must, therefore, develop him/herself from the outside in (i.e., from the physical plane to the spiritual dimension).

Silat Kebatinan

Not unlike the corporeal practice of silat, the acquisition of silat kebatinan (e.g., mystical/spiritual training after mastery of the physical art) is gained through a series of progressive stages. As noted by Maliszewski (1992: 28), "[M]ethods of spiritual development resemble the path of silat in many ways, such as . . . moving from external concerns in the world to inner development, importance given to the role of guru, and the significance attributed to moral and ethical conduct." With silat kebatinan, the focus is placed not on physical skills but on inner development which at once transcends the material world and controls it. Again, this mystical path is not necessarily concurrent with all kebatinan movements. Rather, it is determined by the individual aliran or variant thereof to which one subscribes.

The path of silat kebatinan stresses the *rasa* (ind., jav., intuitive inner feeling) and *sujud* (ind., jav., self-surrender). To effect these qualities the practitioner rids himself of earthly habits and desires by emptying his ego so as to be open to receive the divine presence of God, the revelation of the divine residing within the heart (*batin*) (Maliszewski, 1992). The most important attribute of the pesilat is the ethical understanding of his every action. The pesilat fears the outcome of being put in a position of ever having to employ his deadly martial skills. As a result of possessing and developing these God-given fighting abilities, the pesilat, through the prayers associated with silat kebatinan, always holds sacred the qualities of being gracious and merciful.

In silat kebatinan, the *pikiran* (ind., mind) and the *batin* (heart) are never separated. In silat kebatinan, the body (external) is believed to be controlled by the mind, while the feelings (internal) are controlled by the heart. It is generally believed that, if negativity is cultivated from the onset, then the pesilat will be in constant conflict with himself. The biggest war is that which is fought within. If the pesilat can control the internal war, then the external poses no real threat to him. From another perspective, the innerman is conceived of as a microcosm (jav., *jagat cilik*) of the macrocosm (jav., *jagat gede*) that is life (Mulder, 1970b). The practitioner of kebatinan seeks to cultivate the true self (jav., *ingsun gede*), achieving harmony and ultimately unity with this all-encompassing principle (jav., *manunggaling kawula-Gusti*) as well as with his origin and his destination (jav., *sangkan-paran*). In this final process, the adept becomes one with ultimate reality (Mulder, 1970a). While the attainment of proficiency in corporeal silat may seem rather rudimentary, the path of silat kebatinan is quite strenuous. Overcoming one's attachment to the outward aspects of existence (ind., jav., *lahir*) is no easy attainment and may involve ascetic practices (jav., *tapa*) such as fasting, prayer, mediation (particularly visual concentrative techniques), sexual abstinence, remaining awake throughout the night, or retreating to the mountains and into caves (Maliszewski, 1992). Since this type of practice requires a mode of perseverance and discipline that is demanding, it can be understood why kebatinan is left to the final stage of silat training—the training environment of a *pendekar*[7] (ind., malay, fighter; old jav., skilled duelist, spiritualist).

A common attribute associated with Southeast Asian martial culture is the combination of physical training and occult skills (Draeger, 1972; Draeger & Smith, 1980). These skills include qualities such as invulnerability (jav., *kekebalan*), the ability to fight reflexively, without thought (jav., *kadigdayan*), the ability to withstand a dagger's thrust into the abdomen, and the ability to push or kill at a distance (Draeger, 1972; Draeger & Smith, 1980; Maliszewski, 1987, 1992; Sheikh, 1994). Often, these skills are closely related with the possession of power objects (ind., *jimat*).

These amulets may take the form of gemstones, carriages, birds, or *kris* (jav., dual-edged, serpentine dagger). Whatever the object, its power (jav., *kasekten*) has been attributed to the infusion of living spirit (Stange, 1980). There is one kris in particular, known as the *taming sari* (ind., shielded fruit), which is currently in the possession of the Malayan royal courts. This kris was purportedly made by a man's bare hands, without the aid of water to reduce its temperature, for the legendary Huang Tuah[8] during the fourteenth century. This dagger is said to possess its rightful heir with the spirit power of this culture hero, thus making the holder invincible in battle[9] (Draeger & Smith, 1980; Sheikh, 1994).

Huang Tuah is credited as the bearer of the first kris which was said to have no sheath or scabbard. He considered an enemy's body its only sheath.

Perhaps the most demanding aspect of martial training is the necessity of one's strict adherence to prayer. Primary to the prayer is one's unconditional commitment to God. This commitment is made by way of a vow through the guidance of one's guru. Pesilat and pendekar alike view the consequence of not fully committing to the vow as a serious breach with God.[10] These vows might include the reciting of 70,000 phrases from the Koran, twelve per day. This recitation can not be taken lightly for if one is up to 60,000 recitations and forgets to continue the next day he must begin all over again with phrase one.[11]

To this end, in some systems of silat, breathing is related to meditative aspects which stem from the heart (*batin*) whereas other systems stress the region of the abdomen just below the navel (Draeger, 1972; Draeger & Chambers, 1972). The emphasis placed upon "energy" or "inner power" (ind., *ilmu kebatinan*; jav., *ngelmu kebatinan*) will also vary from one system to another (Maliszewski, 1992). The purification achieved through tapa may lead to *semadi* (skt., *samadhi*; jav., ind., *samadi*), a state of mind best described as "world-detached concentration where one is open to receive divine guidance and knowledge and ultimately the revelation of the mystery of life, origin and destiny" (Maliszewski, 1992: 29). Semadi meditation may be practiced as part of one's silat kebatinan for the express purpose of (1) developing a destructive aim by means of magic, (2) attain a specific positive goal for which greatly enhanced power is needed, (3) experience revelation of the mystery of existence, and (4) achieve ultimate deliverance from all earthly desires (Mangkunagara VII of Surakarta, 1957).

Indeed, the final stage in silat training is kebatinan—a metaphysical, supernatural, phenomenological state of being. Without the acquisition of kebatinan, one's silat is said to be incomplete. Moreover, it seems that the pendekar becomes a spiritualist first and a pesilat second. This is understood to mean that the true possession of kebatinan places one beyond the material realms and cultural constraints of this world. Unlike in the West where the Cartesian split exists between mind, body, and spirit, religious practices permeate all aspects of culture and existence in the East. Even in the more base forms of physical expression (e.g., fighting skills) the role accorded to kebatinan was paramount. In the West, the impact of silat has only stressed the physical-skill component of a rich tradition. The purpose of this paper has been to document the importance of kebatinan in general and to acquaint the reader with a brief overview illustrating the pervasiveness of these religious-mystical beliefs in the Southeast Asian martial culture at large.

Notes

1 For a good overview of a number of kebatinan variants found in Java, see Clifford Geertz, *The Religion of Java* (1960). For a detailed discussion on the variants found within aliran kebatinan, see Neils Mulder's *Aliran Kebatinan* as an expression of the Javanese worldview (1970b).

2 Sheikh Shamsuddin (personal communication, March 12, 1994) is a Malaysian-born instructor of Malay Silat Seni Gayong. The name of this art form, when translated, describes the progression of this indigenous fighting form. Silat refers to the corporeal combative form; *seni* is the fine-tuning or artistic expression of silat; *gayong* is the spiritual dimension, which encompasses the practice of various kebatinan.

3 Video footage of various silat kebatinan were provided for me by *mahaguru* (ind., jav., master teacher) Herman Suwanda of the silat Mande Muda style of Bandung, Indonesia, and by Dr. Michael Maliszewski. These tapes include demonstrations of silat masters chewing and swallowing glass, chewing sharp razor blades, cutting tree leaves and wood with various daggers and swords and hacking their own bodies, as well as rubbing flaming torches on their bare skin, all producing no apparent adverse effects.

4 Sulaiman Sharif (personal communications, 1989–1991) stresses that the practice of dzikir breathing is an essential element of the *gayong* (spiritual) stage of Malaysian silat practice. Sulaiman Sharif is a Malaysian-born master of Silat Seni Gayong and head of the Silat Seni Gayong America Association.

5 Neils Mulder (1970b) describes Javanism as follows: "The Javanese Weltanshauung [Worldview] . . . is based on the conviction of the essential unity of all existence. This worldview is more encompassing than religion: it views human existence with a cosmological context, making life itself a religious experience. In this view of life it is not possible to separate the religious from the nonreligious elements; human existence is inescapably related to supernature and it is senseless to sharply distinguish between here and now and the beyond and timeless" (105).

6 For a detailed study of the social, cultural, spiritual components and symbolism of the wayang kulit see Mangkunagoro VII of Surakarta's data paper, *On the Wayang Kulit (purwa) and Its Symbolic and Mystical Elements* (1957).

7 In silat kebatinan, the title of *pendekar* connotes one who is a spiritualist and leader or champion who has obtained an understanding of true (inner) knowledge, believed to be derived from a Menangkabau expression, *pandai akal*, literally, "ability and mind"; or *andeka*, derived from *adhika*, skt., "more, surpassing in quality," integrated into Malay, here referring to a kind of supernatural power possessed by a *dato* (ind., chief) (Chambers & Draeger, 1978; Draeger, 1972,

Maliszewski, 1987, 1992).

[8] Huang Tuah is credited as the bearer of the first kris which was said to have no sheath or scabbard. Tuah considered an enemy's body its only sheath (Draeger & Smith, 1980; Sheikh, 1994).

[9] For this perspective in relation to the kris, see Draeger (1972), O'Connor (1975), Garrett & Solymon (1978), and Hamzuri (1984).

[10] Sulaiman Sharif, personal communications, 1989–1991.

[11] Sheikh Shamsuddin, personal communication, March 15, 1994.

Languages

Arabic = arb.
Indonesian = ind.
Sanskrit = skt.
Javanese = jav.

References

Chambers, Q., & Draeger, D. (1978). *Javanese silat: The fighting art of perisai diri*. Tokyo: Kodansha.

Draeger, D. (1972). *Weapons and fighting arts of the Indonesian archipelago*. Tokyo: Charles E. Tuttle.

Draeger, D., & Smith, R. (1980). *Comprehensive Asian fighting arts*. Tokyo: Kodansha.

Bronronwen, G., & Bronronwen, B. (1978). *The world of the Javanese kris*. Honolulu: Asian Arts Press.

Geertz, C. (1960). *The religion of Java*. London: Collier-Macmillan Ltd.

Hamzuri, D. (1984). *Keris*. Jakarta: Penerbit Djambatan.

Keyes, C., & Daniels, E. (1983). *Karma: An anthropological inquiry*. Berkeley: University of California Press.

Maliszewski, M. (1987). Martial arts: An overview. In Mircea Eliade (Ed.), *The Encyclopedia of Religion* (Vol. 9, pp. 224–228). New York: Macmillan.

Maliszewski, M. (1992). Medical, healing and spiritual components of Asian martial arts: a preliminary field study exploration. *Journal of Asian Martial Arts, 1*(2), 24–57.

Mangkunagara VII of Surakarta, K.G.P.A.A. (1957). On the wayang kulit (purwa) and its symbolic and mystical elements (Claire Holt, Trans.) (Data Paper, No. 27). Ithaca, New York: Cornell University, Southeast Asia Program, Department of Far Eastern Studies.

Mulder, N. (1970a). A comparative note on the Thai and the Javanese worldview as expressed by religious practice and belief. *Journal of the Siam Society, 58*(2), 79–85.

Mulder, N. (1970b). Aliran kebatinan as an expression of the Javanese worldview. *Journal of Southeast Asian Studies, 1*(2), 105–114.

Mulder, N. (1982). Abangan Javanese religious thought and practice. *Bijdragen tot de Tool-, Land- en Volkenkunde, 139,* 260–267.

O'Connor, S. (1975). Iron working as spiritual inquiry in the Indonesian archipelago. *History of Religions, 14*(3), 173–190.

Stange, P. (1980). The sumarah movement in Javanese mysticism. (Doctoral dissertation, University of Wisconsin, Madison, Department of History, 1980).

Wiley, M. (1993). Silat seni gayong: Seven levels of self-defense. *Journal of Asian Martial Arts, 3*(4), 76–95.

The Pauleh Tinggi Ceremony in West Sumatra: Martial Arts, Magic, and Male Bonding

by Kirstin Pauka, Ph.D.

Two senior Ulu Ambek masters from
different schools pair up for a performance.
Note their eyes look upward
and do not focus on their partner.

Photographs courtesy of K. Pauka.

The Pauleh Tinggi is a unique ceremony of the Minangkabau ethnic group in the coastal Pariaman area in West Sumatra, Indonesia. It features all-male performances and stylized competitions in the local martial arts style called Ulu Ambek, which relies heavily on the use of magic. The execution of the Pauleh Tinggi is a truly exceptional occurrence. The one I witnessed in June, 994, was only the third such event in this century.[1] Two previous ceremonies were held in 1936 and in 1967, neither of which was documented. This ceremony is carried out in honor of the ancestors and elders, celebrating the unbroken line of clan traditions (*adat*). Its purpose is to foster good relations between the male leaders of the ten main clans of the region.

Before a Pauleh Tinggi ceremony can take place, all disputes among the ten participating clans must be settled. It is the obligation of the respective male clan elders to hold meetings; find out about any quarrel, dispute or other disruption of harmony between the clans; discuss it with them; and find a solution based on consensus. This tradition creates a strong bond among the male leaders of the clans. The (re)establishment of harmony through a concerted effort by the male elders is celebrated by the Pauleh Tinggi ceremony.[2]

Ulu Ambek is a martial arts form indigenous to the Pariaman area. Still mostly practiced in secrecy, it is very rarely displayed publicly, except in the Pauleh Tinggi.[3] Any public display can only occur with the permission of the clan leader (Harun, 1992: 67). Its most outstanding feature is the avoidance of actual physical contact that is typical of silat, the other indigenous martial art form of Sumatra (Draeger, 1972). In Ulu Ambek, magic powers are used to prevent or overcome an attack. True masters can extend their magic powers to their students and protect them against harm. The relationship between master and student is very close. The male-bonding here happens between generations, whereas the bonding among the clan elders involves males of approximately the same age group. The young students are selected by the teacher and become his disciples. This extremely strong bond between the younger performers and their teachers is apparent throughout the performances of Ulu Ambek. The students are very respectful and reverential towards their older teachers, and in return the teachers show their support by remaining close to the stage, while chanting mantras and calling through stylized yells for the protection of their disciples. This appears to be a standard practice in Ulu Ambek (Cordes, 1990: 229) and is omnipresent in the Pauleh Tinggi ceremony.

The Chain of Events

The preparations for this auspicious event involve the entire community and stretch over twelve months. The actual construction of the ceremonial stage area and the decoration of the entire marketplace start two weeks prior to the opening night. The ceremony itself lasts three days and three nights, followed by twelve more days of other, less formal entertainment for the general public.

Only members of the hosting clan participate in the events of the first night. This is considered as initiation for the performance space and a warm-up for the participants in preparation for the arrival of the guests the following night. The stage is inaugurated by the highest ranking clan elders of the hosting clan in Sicincin city. Elaborate ceremonial speeches in the indigenous language of the Minangkabau people (*bahaso minang*) precede the Tari Sampai, a very slow and dignified ceremonial dance based on Ulu Ambek movements, which is executed by the two highest ranking elders. This dance is followed by more official speeches in the Indonesian state language (*bahasa indonesia*). Thereafter, circular dances called Randai Ulu Ambek, also based on Ulu Ambek movements, are performed for several hours by groups of seven to nine performers, followed by several more hours of pure Ulu Ambek, which is performed by only two people.

On the second night, the invited delegations from the nine surrounding districts (*nagari*) arrive and are welcomed with a linear martial arts dance called *tari galombang*, based on the movement repertoire of Ulu Ambek, but faster paced. This dance is performed outside the stage area, in between the gate of the marketplace and the gate of the stage building in the open marketplace.

From here the guests are guided into the stage area, where elaborate ceremonial speeches in *bahaso minang* are exchanged between the host and the guest clan elders. The host clan then formally opens the stage with the circular Randai Ulu Ambek, and then each of the nine guest clans proceed to perform its own version of Randai Ulu Ambek.

On the third day, Ulu Ambek between the members of the host clan and members of the guest clans is performed starting in the afternoon, followed by more Randai Ulu Ambek in the evening and night. These all-night performances, lasting until approximately five o'clock in the morning, are attended by hundreds of men and boys and only a few women, who observe the ceremony from farther away, outside the fence. On the following day, the Pauleh Tinggi is formally ended with final Ulu Ambek performances and ceremonial closing speeches by the elders.

The Performance Space

For the Pauleh Tinggi, the public marketplace is divided and transformed into a reception area and a performance space. The reception area is delineated by decorations consisting of a large, five-meter-high and three-meter-wide, decorated bamboo arc at the entrance into the marketplace and bamboo poles with flags and tassels along the sidelines of the place. The performance space is created at the back end of the market in the form of a large, rectangularly roofed stage.

The stage platform consists of three horizontal layers: a ground layer of coconut trunks, perpendicular to them a middle layer of bamboo poles sliced into halves, and the top layer consisting of thin bamboo planks tied together with ropes (Fig. 1). Due to the arrangement of the hollow bamboo halves and the light and rather loose upper bamboo strips, this type of floor proves to be very elastic and resonant, a quality that emphasizes steps and stomps, prominent movement patterns of Ulu Ambek. This central platform is surrounded on four sides by a sitting area at ground level, covered with mats. This area is closed off from the outside by a knee-high, decorated bamboo fence and is roofed over (Fig. 2).

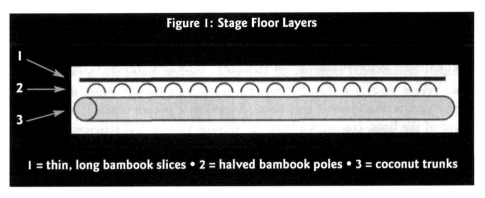

Figure 1: Stage Floor Layers

1 = thin, long bambook slices • 2 = halved bambook poles • 3 = coconut trunks

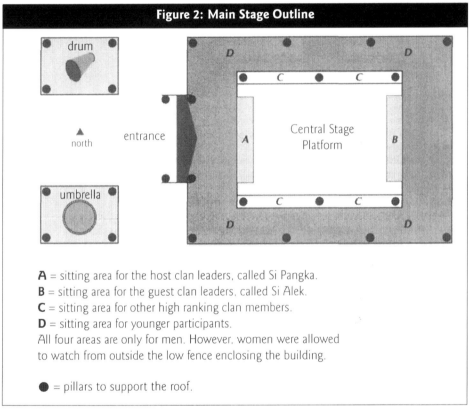

Figure 2: Main Stage Outline

drum

north

entrance

umbrella

D

C   C

A   Central Stage Platform   B

C   C

D   D

A = sitting area for the host clan leaders, called Si Pangka.
B = sitting area for the guest clan leaders, called Si Alek.
C = sitting area for other high ranking clan members.
D = sitting area for younger participants.
All four areas are only for men. However, women were allowed to watch from outside the low fence enclosing the building.

● = pillars to support the roof.

The seating arrangement inside the stage area is very specific and strictly follows the Minangkabau clan traditions (*adat*) for the seating regulations in the traditional Minangkabau house (*rumah gadang*). Accordingly, it is mandatory to honor the guests by seating them on the inner side of the house. Therefore, the hosts occupy the seating area closer to the entrance side of the stage area.

The roof is held up by six vertical bamboo poles placed around the inner platform and twelve placed along the outside fence. Four crossbeams support the thatching.[4] The entrance has a small protruding roof in the traditional style of Minangkabau architecture: an arch with a pointed tip. To the left and right side of the entrance are two small huts. The right one houses the insignia of Minangkabau adat: several long swords, a metal cerano vessel, a banner and a highly ornamented cushion, all arranged together under the royal, ceremonial, yellow umbrella. The left hut houses the big tabuah drum that is normally kept at the mosque and used to announce prayer times. The arrangement of the huts, containing insignia relevant to adat and religion, is intended to show that Minangkabau traditions and Islam exist in harmony. Both huts are thatched and enclosed by colorful banners. Inside the main stage area, several more banners are hung under the roof above the central stage area.[5]

An interesting additional feature are two mirrors that hang above the seating areas "A" and "B." I obtained several explanations for the presence of these mirrors, some informants stating that the mirrors themselves are endowed with magic powers and are placed over the stage to protect the participants. Others see them as merely decorative objects. On a practical level, they are supposed to enable the performers to "see behind their backs." The stage area basically is unaltered throughout the three days of the ceremony, except for slight changes to accommodate the musicians on the first and second day.

Performance Features of the Ceremony

In the Pauleh Tinggi ceremony, an otherwise very secretive martial arts form is displayed publicly. However, the participants stay inside the enclosed performance space and do not interact with the general public, which watches from outside the fence. It seems that the inside of the stage building exists in a different sphere altogether.[6] The strong bonds between the clan elders who share the responsibility for the harmonious flow of the event and the bonds between each teacher and his students due to their intimate training relationship create an atmosphere of enclosure and separate the participants from the ordinary space of all other onlookers. The level of concentration and seriousness is constantly high, because any kind of disturbance in the flow of the ceremony could possibly lead to a disarray of the clan relations.

Besides the standard Ulu Ambek, three other martial forms, based on a similar repertoire of movements, are displayed in the Pauleh Tinggi: Randai Ulu Ambek, Tari Galombang, and Tari Sampai, all of which shall be discussed in detail below.

Ulu Ambek

The name *Ulu Ambek* literally means "stop at the peak" or "stop before the peak" and can be interpreted as referring to the preemptive–defensive quality of this unique martial art. Its most outstanding characteristic is that there is rarely any physical contact between the players although they execute martial attack and defense moves comparable to the punches, strikes and kicks seen in silat or other Asian martial arts.[7] An attack is "stopped before it peaks" or makes contact. To accomplish this, the true combat takes place on a non-physical level, referred to as the *raso* ("feeling") level.

Ulu Ambek performed by two participants from the same clan and school.

To master Ulu Ambek, the practitioners have to learn and develop what they call *ilmu batin* or *kebatinan* ("magic skill or power"). In the beginning of the training, the teacher extends his own magic power to his students who have not yet acquired the magic skills for themselves. Each student has to entrust himself to his teacher to be guided by him through physical and spiritual training. Only very few students are capable of doing so and the teachers are very selective. The concept of this magic power is very illusive and not readily described by the practitioners. However, during the Pauleh Tinggi performances it is evident that an important aspect of the practice of Ulu Ambek is the development of a perception that is dependent on peripheral vision. Further developing these concrete physical skills might lead to a sharpened sixth sense, very good intuition, and to what is called "seeing beyond" on a more metaphysical level.[8]

Ulu Ambek is always performed by only two men. Their performance is accompanied by chanting that starts before they enter the stage and by yells and shouts from other spectators during the performance. The students respect for their elders is apparent in their behavior prior to the performance. Upon entering the stage area, each one kneels before his teacher, folds his hands and receives a blessing in the form of a gentle touch of the hands and a murmured mantra. Then both performers proceed to greet other elders and teachers in a similar fashion before stepping into the stage center. Here, they repeat their greeting gesture in four directions by alternately extending their arms and then covering the face briefly with both hands. The players then take their positions in the southwest and northeast corners of the stage respectively. Down the middle of the stage area is an invisible line that is not crossed during the first segment of Ulu Ambek. Both partners move around in their half of the stage, executing slow-paced movements interrupted by occasional fast stomping of the feet, which is amplified by the resonant stage floor. The sequence before the line is crossed is referred to as *betina*.[9] Both performers move in unison. Although they do not use the exact same body positions or moves, their movements are similar in terms of overall posture and the more detailed positioning of the feet, hands, and angle of the head. What is more striking is that they precisely synchronize their movements in terms of tempo rhythm and with a similar overall flow. This might be explained by the fact that the performers have trained together for a long time and are very familiar with the sequences and form. However, in regard to the ceremony I observed, the synchronicity was even more amazing on the second night, when two players from different villages were paired up. They had supposedly not performed together for years, if at all, and still their movements blended exactly.

The structure of an Ulu Ambek encounter is very similar throughout the entire ceremony. Following the first section in which both performers remain in their half of the stage (*betina*), they get closer to the center line, and as soon as one crosses over it, they enter into the sequence called *jantan* (male), in which they start to exchange between five and eight attack and defense movements with the hands and arms. With his blows the attacker drives his partner on a diagonal line into one corner of the stage. Reaching it, the "trapped" partner turns his back on the attacker, seemingly oblivious to the attacks and, extending some kind of energy that stops the attacker, drives him away. This sequence is repeated three times. They then change roles and the other performer starts to attack, drives his partner into a corner, and then backs away as soon as his partner turns his back on him. The performance ends with both partners exchanging another formal greeting with each other and the audience. Then a metal vessel (*cerano*) covered with an embroidered cloth is brought onstage by a young boy. Both performers bow to the cerano one final time as a sign of respect for the ancestors and elders, and then leave the stage.

The physical techniques used in Ulu Ambek consist mainly of hand tech-niques. No kicks, leg sweeps or other leg techniques were observed. Occasionally they execute strikes with the head or shoulders. The main attacking moves are sideways or backwards elbow strikes, punches with the fists or palm heels, poking with one finger, and slaps to both ears of the partner with open palms. In the preparatory phase before a strike, the hands are often above head level, in front of the face or slightly to the side, with fingers apart and quivering. Or, when not engaged in striking, the right fist often rests against the open palm of the left hand, or the performers place their own hands or arms close to their torso or thighs, frequently even touching their own body.

The stances range from upright stances with feet close together to *kudo-kudo* (medium-wide horse stances with feet about two shoulder widths apart) to very low crouches. In most of these stances, the weight is unevenly distributed between both legs and often the legs were trembling in a controlled manner while inching further apart into a wider stance.

Tari Sampai

The *Tari Sampai* ("delivery dance") is the ceremonial opening dance performed by the two highest-ranking datuk of the host clan.[10] Both performers are dressed in full ceremonial dress consisting of long black pants (*galembong*), a long-sleeved shirt, a hip cloth and sash, a shoulder sash, and a headdress called *saluak*. Upon entering the stage area with slow dignified steps, they start their performance with the *garak sembah*, the greeting sequence typical of Ulu Ambek. Both performers walk the entire stage area while alternately extending both arms diagonally (the fingers pointing upwards and apart) and then bending both arms and covering the entire face with both hands. This greeting gesture is first executed with both performers facing each other, then repeated several times in all directions towards the spectators, and then one last time while they again faced each other. After this last greeting, they both step back to take their places in the northeast and southwest corners of the stage. From there they start to dance to the accompaniment of an orchestra, their feet and hand movements accentuated by the sound of the large tabuah drum.

In the first sequence, both men remain in their respected halves of the stage as in the standard performance of Ulu Ambek, not crossing over the centerline, which is marked by a small, rectangular, fine straw mat. Their basic posture is a high stance with the center of weight mainly above the back foot with both feet never more than one shoulder width apart. The torso is kept upright. Two of the most intriguing features of this dance are the finger and the eye movements. One or more fingers frequently tremble, often barely noticeably. The eyes are turned away from the partner to either the left or right upper corner. Both these features are explained as showing that the dancers are performing magic.

The two highest, ranking clan elders perform
the Tari Sampai to inaugurate the stage.

The term "magic" is used by performers and other informants in a rather broad sense. In this specific opening dance, the dancers' magic is believed to extend as a protective shield over the entire ceremonial event and ensure its success. The finger trembling is explained as an outward sign of their sensitivity and awareness. In a sense, they are scanning for possible disturbances and dispelling them, using their hands (and possibly their entire body) as antennas. After the initial movement sequence, during which each dancer remains in his half of the stage area, they move towards the center, and each dancer picks up one piece of long batik fabric that has been placed on the straw mat beforehand. Grabbing the fabric delicately at the edges with just two fingers of each hand, each dancer stretches it between his hands in front of his face. Continuing his slow and evenly paced steps back and forth across the stage, each proceeds to move his piece of fabric diagonally in front of his body, both fabrics intersecting in the center, thereby symbolizing crossed swords. The cloth is used instead of real weapons for two reasons. It is considered a sign of politeness towards each other and the spectators. Also, the use of the fabric is perceived as more aesthetically pleasing. Throughout the entire Tari Sampai, the performers move in a restrained and slow, yet intense and concentrated fashion, appearing very dignified.

Two clan elders open the Pauleh Tinggi
ceremony by performing the Tari Sampai.

Randai Ulu Ambek

Immediately after the opening dance (*Tari Sampai*), nine practitioners perform what is called Randai Ulu Ambek, a circular martial arts dance led by their teacher. Traditionally, this practice is the basic teaching arrangement for a larger group of students. In it, the students closely imitate the proper execution, pace, and intensity of their teacher's movements. Through this training, the students develop a strong bond with their teacher, who extends and passes his power to his disciples.

The Randai form is considered the initiation into the true art of Ulu Ambek and students have to master the group form first before they are allowed to engage in it individually. As part of the Pauleh Tinggi ceremony, the Randai is accompanied by a specific chant sung by two singers and a chorus formed by the other Ulu Ambek players sitting around the stage. The song contains descriptions of how nature is supposed to function as a teacher in every aspect of the practitioners' lives. The lyrics are frequently accompanied by nonsense syllables, shouts and yells. Before starting the practice, each of the participants goes through a lengthy greeting routine, kneeling in front of every high-ranking elder on the stage platform, holding hands and then covering his face with both his hands for an instant. All wear black gelambang pants, a batik hip cloth, a batik headdress wrapped in a specific fashion (*destar*), and a shirt or T-shirt.

Randi Ulu Ambek.

Again, the most outstanding physical features during the martial performances are the wiggling fingers, the eyes intensely focused diagonally upwards, and the overall high tension of the body throughout the performance. The synchronization of the movements of all group members is outstanding. A strong spiritual connection between the leader and the students is apparent, and the level of concentration and focus is very high. Three different types of movements are prevalent: slow moving, evenly paced sequences; complete freezes; and sudden, explosive moves. The main flow of evenly paced moves is broken by a few sudden, wide-spaced, explosive moves that often lead to a momentary freeze. Sometimes the freeze ends with a sudden initial move that serves as a bridge into the slow moving sequence again. The poses that are held for several seconds in a complete freeze highlight the good balance and focus of the performers (for example, freezes on one leg, or with uneven weight distribution on both legs, or in low crouches with one leg extended). Sudden moves out of a freeze include swift body turns, rotating flapping hands over the head, snapping into a palm-heel block or other blocks. To accentuate position changes, performers often stomp one or both feet hard on the stage floor, creating a loud and resonant sound due to the special construction of the floor. This stomping typically occurs out of a stance in which the performer stands on one leg with the other raised high, the knee bent in a ninety-degree angle. It is executed with full force and a flat foot to produce the correct sound (loud and sharp) and to avoid injury. Besides these sudden bursts of fast motion, the other eye-catching exception to the even pace of the movements is the almost continuous trembling of the fingers.

Randi Ulu Ambek performed by members
of the host clan. Note the mirror overhead.

The performers are intensely concentrated, completely oblivious to extraneous occurrences, completely focused on the group leader and their own movement. At times, they seem as if they are physically and mentally moved by the leader. In a later interview, this perception was confirmed by one of the participants, who described his experience as being guided and moved by the teacher's powers. While their focus is entirely on the leader, their eyes are not. Instead, they are almost always gazing beyond: beyond their own fingers, beyond the teacher and beyond the immediate stage area. Their gazes sweep through space like beams of light, never stopping on a specific object or person. In this "unfocused focus" it becomes evident and visible that Ulu Ambek training aims at the sharpening of peripheral vision and an ability to "see beyond" place and time in a more general and mystic way.

At the performance I observed, the same Randai Ulu Ambek group performed the same circle dance on the second night after all the guest parties had arrived. This was followed by very similar performances of Randai Ulu Ambek by the guests.[11]

Tari Galombang

The Tari Galombang is performed as a welcoming dance for the guests on the second night. The musical instruments of the adok orchestra (consisting of several metal gongs and kettles and several different-size drums) are all placed in the small hut on the left side outside the stage. The musicians seat themselves facing the large entrance arch on the opposite side of the market square, under which the guest delegations make their first appearance.

Tari Galombong welcoming dance in the Pauleh Tinggi.

As soon as all members of one delegation are lined up under the arch, the music starts and a group of six male dancers perform the traditional Tari Galombang, composed of movements from the Ulu Ambek repertoire but faster paced. It is performed in a linear formation (Fig. 3). The host delegation of dancers proceed towards the guest delegation in a short dance that lasts less than two minutes. It begins with the specific Ulu Ambek greeting gesture in four directions starting towards the back (where the elders of the host clan are located), then towards the guests, and then towards the general audience who line both sides of the pathway. Moving slowly forwards and backwards with Ulu Ambek steps, the host delegation proceeds towards the entrance arch slowly. The music and movements accelerate toward the end and climax with hand claps by the dancers and a salute shot from a rifle. After this, the dancers rush to the guests with extended arms. Following them is a young boy carrying a cerano vessel (containing betel nut, cigarettes, and other offerings, a traditional Minangkabau custom to honor guests), which is presented to the leader of the guest delegation.

After the guests are led into the stage area to their assigned seats, the Tari Gelombang performers return to their place outside the stage to await the next delegation. At the performance I observed, the guests arrived over a period of three and a half hours, and for some of the later ones only four dancers were left to perform. Three of the guest delegations respond to the greeting dance by performing a similar dance, synchronizing their movements to the ones of the host group in terms of tempo, rhythm, and positioning, and both groups simultaneously climax in the final hand clapping highlighted by the rifle salute.[12] These spontaneous interactions create intriguing spatial formations and dynamics and delight the audiences tremendously. It is also perceived as a good sign for the successful course of the ceremony.

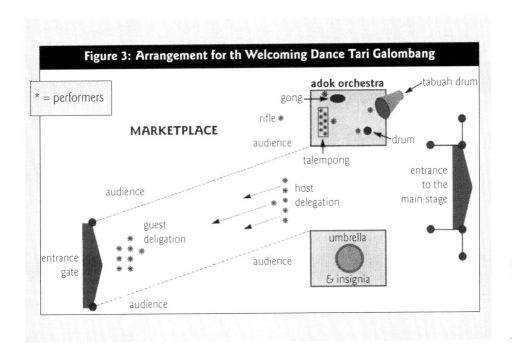

Figure 3: Arrangement for th Welcoming Dance Tari Galombang

Music

All performances are accompanied by music. On the first night, the seating area "A" in the central stage area is utilized by five musicians playing in the orchestra. This orchestra consists of various drums, gongs and bronze kettles and produces a unique, lively sound. The feature instrument of this orchestra is the *adok*, a large, flat, one-sided drum, along with a smaller version of it called *rabana*. A very large, oblong, two-headed drum, called *tabuah*, is mounted in a wooden stand with the larger drum head facing diagonally upwards. It is beaten with a thick stick. The tabuah keeps the basic beat while the other drums play variations of the rhythm.

The only melodic instrument is an approximately 120-year-old talempong consisting of five bronze kettles suspended in a wooden frame low above the ground. Two gongs, one large one (called *aguang*) suspended from a beam, and a smaller, hand-held one (called *momongan*) complete the orchestra. Except for the tabuah and the aguang player, all musicians are seated on the ground.

87

Musicians for the opening ceremony, Tari Sampai.
Note the female players in white headdresses.

On the opening night, the orchestra is led by an older woman who opens the ceremony by performing the *tapuah setado*, beating the large aguang gong three times.[13] After this, the musicians play twelve pieces lasting about thirty minutes. The earlier ones are played in a slow and dignified tempo with following pieces at an ever increasing speed until the music finally culminates in a rapid and exciting finale. The musicians stop abruptly and the large drum is beaten three times before the Tari Sampai is performed. This dance and all following performances are accompanied by the orchestra. Only the large tabuah drum is placed in the hut outside the stage area after the opening night. Considered precious heirlooms (*pusako*), the metal instruments are formally returned to the owners (the village elders of Sungai Asam, just outside Sicincin) in a procession after the Pauleh Tinggi ceremony is over.

Accompanying Events of the Pauleh Tinggi

On the second day, pig and bird hunting takes place in the surrounding forests, in which most members of the hosting clan participate. The fourth night features competitions of Silat Kumango, Sitaralak, and Mangguang (the three main silat styles in the Pariaman area besides Ulu Ambek). This fourth night opens with Randai Silat, during which silat is performed in a circular fashion, accompanied by flute music (*saluang*). It is followed by silat played by two performers, again until five a.m. The next day, silat performances continue from around noon and then climax in *silat pisau* (silat with knives) starting around five p.m. Silat pisau is only played by the most advanced practitioners.

Two days of silat competition and eight nights of *indang* dancing are followed by a seated dance accompanied by drumming and religious chants. Each of the four main villages of the Sicincin area play two consecutive nights. These events are carried out in a less formal fashion, and the stage area is accessible to the general public including women.

Musicians for the welcoming dance Tari Galombang. The metal gongs are called talempong and the big flat drum is called an adok.

Conclusions

The main objective of the Pauleh Tinggi is to secure harmony and balance in the community. This is achieved on several levels: first, amongst the members of each martial arts school, clan and participating village; second, among clans and among villages; third, between traditional Minangkabau customs and Islam; and fourth, between the world of the living and the world of the ancestors.

First, each clan and/or village has specific responsibilities before and during the event for which all members are expected to engage in *gotong-royong* (working together on a communal project).[14] The work and responsibilities are divided very precisely among the clans and subclans. The host clan is responsible for the planning of the entire event and for the erection of the stage building.[15] Other (guest) clans are in charge of providing the materials for the stage structure and the other decorations of the marketplace. One subclan is specifically responsible for supplying the coconut tree logs for the stage floor; a second one for the bamboo cover layer; a third one for the bamboo pillars; a fourth one for the roof beams; a fifth one for the roof thatching; and so on (all of which helped split the labor and costs among the participants). The decorative banners for the stage roof are provided by the family of the clan elder, and the instruments of the adok orchestra are taken care of by another subclan of the host. This way, most of the male population of the area is engaged in the preparation of the event, which creates a strong sense of community.

Each participating Ulu Ambek school is expected to be well prepared and have enough initiated participants to partake in the performances. This demands long and frequent training sessions, which in turn create closer relations among all the members.[16]

On the second level, communication and relations between the host clan and the guest clans are crucial and geared towards strengthening the bond among the male leaders. For all stages of the ceremony, including the preparations, specific and proper decorum is prescribed and followed meticulously. For example, the formal invitations to all participating clans have to be delivered by a delegation specifically chosen from the host clan. This delegation walks in a procession to the house of the clan elder of each clan, bringing with them a cerano vessel with offerings of sirieh leaves, betel nut and tobacco. According to Minangkabau customs, the delegation is not allowed to make prior arrangements with the guests for a specific day and time for the meeting. If the elders are not at home or ready to receive the invitation, the delegation has to come back another day and try again.[17] The formal invitation is extended and accepted through polite and formal speeches from both parties (*pidato*) and the exchange of gifts. This way, the intention to participate in the upcoming ceremony is confirmed by both sides.

On the third level, a balance between Minangkabau adat and Islam is desired. The Pauleh Tinggi ceremony at its core is rooted in pre-Islamic, animistic beliefs and ancestor worship, and it features the use of magic as an art form. However, since Islam has been the dominant religion in the region for the past two hundred years, efforts are great to integrate and harmonize both.[18] This is shown in the fact that insignia of both adat and Islam are displayed in the two huts in front of the main stage. Both systems are honored through banners above the stage, and leaders of both systems participate in the elaborate opening and closing ceremonies by giving formal speeches. Each night, performances have to end with the morning prayer call from the mosque shortly before sunrise. Interference with the Muslim worship schedule is avoided.

The last level of harmony and balance to be achieved concerns the ancestors. The cerano is considered a sacred heirloom (called *pusako*) and its presence during the ceremony is an expression of reverence towards the guests and of worship towards the ancestors. The cerano is the main symbolic offering delivered with the formal invitations to each guest clan and is brought out several times during the ceremony: for the opening speeches and inauguration of the stage, for the greeting of the arriving guest clans at the ceremony site, and for the closing speeches.[19] The cerano is indeed present throughout the entire ceremony. After each individual performance of Ulu Ambek and Randai Ulu Ambek, the performers also bow to the cerano which sets on a special place in the seating area of the host clan, next to the elder who is presiding over the performances.

A second cerano vessel is placed in the hut outside the main stage, together with other heirlooms (*pusako*) of the host clan: swords, cushions, and the royal umbrella. These heirlooms have been handed down over generations, like the martial art form of Ulu Ambek, and are also considered sacred. By giving the pusako an honorable space in the performance, the ancestors are honored and the unbroken like of adat is celebrated.[20] Through establishing harmony and balance within each clan, among the clans, between Minangkabau customs and Islam, and with the ancestors, the ceremony in its totality is considered very beneficial for the larger community.

Two questions remain: Why is this ceremony not held more often, and how is it determined when it should be held? One reason it is not held more often is that the practice of Ulu Ambek itself is considered a sacred heirloom and does not have to be displayed publicly to be beneficial. In fact, any public display is treated somewhat apprehensively and the martial artists prefer to practice in secrecy. As a traditional Minangkabau heirloom, Ulu Ambek has to be practiced continuously and handed down; otherwise, it will be forgotten, the line of adat will be broken, the ancestors will be displeased and the new generation will lose its roots in tradition (and no Pauleh Tinggi ceremony would ever take place again). Therefore, the continued practice of Ulu Ambek is the foundation of this structure, and the Pauleh Tinggi is the peak.

Traditionally, the decision to hold the ceremony is made by the clan elders after consultations with other village elders and a *dukun* (traditional doctor and magician). Today, other considerations also influence the planning of the ceremony: the financial situation of the host clan; the presence of enough elders, teachers and students (due to the *merantau* voluntary migration spreading farther and farther away from the home lands, it is hard to bring all members together at anyone time); the right timing with the five-year plans of the Indonesian government (mainly non-interference with election years); and more. According to one of the leading clan elders, Datuk Marajo of Sicincin, it would nowadays be necessary to hold the ceremony more often than in the past because life changes faster for the younger generation and not many elders are left that hold all the knowledge about the ceremony. If they don't teach the younger ones in time (and there are fewer and fewer of the young generation who are interested in learning), the knowledge might be lost forever.

Notes

1. This particular ceremony was held from June 18 to 21, 1994, in the central marketplace in Sicincin, the district capital of Pariaman, in West Sumatra.

2. The Pauleh Tinggi is not performed to re-establish harmony per se or to solve any major conflict. There might very well be no conflict or quarrel at all prior to the ceremony. But if there is, it has to be solved first. If there is a hidden conflict or problem, the elders have to uncover and solve it.

3. Another occasion when Ulu Ambek is displayed publicly is in a less formal ceremony called *Pauleh Rendah*. It is similar in structure and features to Pauleh Tinggi, but it is carried out exclusively by the junior participants, with permission but without the direct involvement of the elders. There is no formal costuming for it and no special performance space. It is simply a forum in which to practice Ulu Ambek.

4. According to the master of ceremonies, Datuk Marajo, the crossbeams symbolize the unity of the people in the Minangkabau adat (traditional customs).

5. The banners included two small, predominantly black ones (*candai*) in honor of the ancestors (*ninik-mamak*) and two bigger ones (*tabir*) richly embroidered in the traditional Minangkabau colors of black, red and gold. These heirlooms of the clan elders are approximately 120 years old. On the far ends of the performance area (above areas "A" and "B" in Figure 2) two smaller plain yellow banners were mounted. Yellow fabric was also wrapped around the inner six pillars and the lower inside edges of the roof. Again, the combination of Minangkabau banners and religious banners was intended to show harmony between these two important aspects of the contemporary Minangkabau society.

6. At one time, a bat flew into the stage building and got trapped in this enclosed sphere. It circled and zigzagged under the roof for over an hour not able to leave the space. This was perceived as a bad omen by the participants. According to local animistic beliefs, bats often host evil spirits and it was feared that the bat might cast evil spells on the performers. Some of the elders started to iterate mantras and were eventually able to chase the bat out.

7. They only touch hands during the greeting ceremony.

8. The fact that mirrors were hung above the sidelines of the stage area seems to contradict the notion that the performers train to see beyond by use of magic and not by use of material devices. However, the mirrors were scarcely used and, if so, only by the younger students, which supports the idea that they were merely symbolic objects of "seeing beyond" and not functional aids.

9. *Betina* literally means "female" and is used to describe a more feminine, beautiful way of moving, as opposed to the *jantan* or "male" sequence in which stronger

combative moves are executed.

[10] Only the two highest-ranking clan elders are entitled to perform this ceremonial dance. According to one of them, they alone hold the knowledge, capability and power to execute this dance properly.

[11] Differences in detail to the previous group included new poses like an extended index finger, pointing to the self or away from the self, and normal walking between movement sequences. This segment of normal walking also appears in Randai Silat, the circular practice formation for other silat styles, as well as in the circular dance formation galombang of the local theater form Randai. Some of the guest groups had new members who were not yet proficient in the form. Their teacher frequently corrected their stances and hand positions. He also slowed down his own movements, especially after body turns so that his students could catch up. Obviously, they hadn't acquired the ability to "see beyond" yet and still relied on direct visual contact with their teacher.

[12] The rifle salute was considered the climax of the welcoming dance. Twice the rifle stalled and no shot came forth. Therefore, in two cases, the whole dance had to be repeated until the salute shot was perceived as satisfactory by the elders.

[13] The opening ceremony was the only time when women—and only two specifically chosen ones—were allowed in the stage area. Generally, the inner area was designated exclusively for men, and women were not even permitted to pass through the area. The only location from which women could observe the ceremony was the public market space outside the fence. The two women chosen to participate in the opening ceremony of the first night were the wife of the master of ceremonies and her daughter. They were seated next to the musicians and on even ground with them. Both wore white costumes and headdresses which, according to tradition, symbolized the ancestors and legendary kings of the past. Awhile after the older woman had initiated the music, both withdrew from the stage.

[14] I was not completely clear how clan and village were separated in terms of their role in this ceremony. Due to the Minangkabau custom of *merantau* (leaving one's home village to gain knowledge, experience, and fortunes somewhere else), the migration rate is very high and often clan members settle down far from their home. For this ceremony many returned home, though.

[15] The town of Sicincin was selected to be the site of the ceremony because the elders of the residing clan there were considered most knowledgeable about the propriety of the execution.

[16] As a foreigner and woman, I had no access to the Ulu Ambek training sessions.

[17] This regulation was never reinforced, though, because the clan elders somehow knew when the delegation planned to deliver the invitation and made sure to

be home.

[18] The Pariaman area is, in fact, the place where Islam was first introduced into Minangkabau society. The arrival of the first disseminators is annually celebrated with the Tabuik festival on the shore of Pariaman town, just an hour drive from Sicincin, the site of the Pauleh Tinggi. These two events actually overlapped for several days during my stay.

[19] The cerano is not really given to the guests. It is the vessel for the gifts of sirieh leaves, betel nut and tobacco, which are taken and consumed by the guests.

[20] To honor the ancestors and elders (*ninik-mamak*) is a crucial element of Minangkabau adat. Each formal speech (*pidato*) has to follow a strict and lengthy pattern of introductory phrases showing respect and gratitude to the ancestors.

References

Cordes, H. (1990). *Pencak silat: Die kampfkunst der minangkabau und ihr kulturelles.* Doctoral dissertation, University of Koln, Germany.

Draeger, D. (1972). *The weapons and fighting arts of the Indonesian archipelago.* Rutland, VT: Charles E. Tuttle Publishing Co.

Harun, C. (1992). *Kesenian randai di minangkabau.* Jakarta: Depdikbud.

index